Between Text
and Community

Between Text and Community

The "Writings" in Canonical Interpretation

DONN F. MORGAN

FORTRESS PRESS   Minneapolis

Cover designer: Mark Stratman

Interior designer: Karen Buck

Library of Congress Cataloging-in-Publication Data

Morgan, Donn F.
    Between text and community : the "writings" in canonical
interpretation / Donn F. Morgan.
        p. cm.
    Includes bibliographical references.
    ISBN 0-8006-2406-8
    1. Bible. O.T. Hagiographa—Criticism, interpretation, etc.
    2. Bible. O.T. Hagiographa—Canon. I. Title.
    BS1308.M67 1990
    221'.042-dc20   89-37528
                                                                        CIP

The paper used in this publication meets the minimum requirements of American National Standard for Information Sciences—Permanence of Paper for Printed Library Materials, ANSI Z329.48-1984. ∞™

Manufactured in the U.S.A.   AF 1-2406

94   93   92   91   90   1   2   3   4   5   6   7   8   9   10

For Alda

Contents

Preface   ix

1. A Canonical View of the Writings   1
   Purpose and Context   1
   The Writings and Canonical Interpretation   5
   Structure and Format   8

2. Canon and Interpretation   11
   Canonical Criticism   11
   Canon and Authority   13
   Community and Text in Dialogue   15
      Community   16
      Text   17
   Scripture and Torah   18
   Methodological Principles and Guidelines   22
      Interpretation of Community   23
      Literary Context, Paradigm, Structure   24
      Theological Principles   26
   Toward a Canonical Hermeneutic for the Writings   27
   Conclusions   28

3. Community Shapes the Text   30
   Scripture and the Writings in the Post-Exilic Period   30
   Scripture   31
      Historical Overview   32
      Torah and Prophets: Development   34
      Tension between Torah and Prophets   37
   The Writings   39
      Sages and Wisdom   40
      Singers and Psalms   42
      Community Builders and Torah-History   44
      Visionaries and Apocalyptic   47
      Storytellers and Diaspora Living   49
   Paradigms for the Future   52
   Community and Text   53
   Toward Canon   55

4. The Text Shapes Community   57
   Scriptural Dialogue in the Writings   57

   Sapiential Literature   59
   Liturgical Literature   61
   Historical Literature   64
   Apocalyptic Literature   66
   Edifying Literature   68
   Conclusions   71

5. Continuity of the Scriptural Pattern   76

   Intertestamental Literature, the New Testament, and Rabbinic
      Literature   76
   Intertestamental Literature   81
   The New Testament Writings   91
   Rabbinic Literature   96
   Canon Revisited   103

6. The Writings as Canon   108

   Canon and Pluralism   111
   Canon and Text   113
   Canon and Community   117
   The Twofold Scriptures of Judaism and Christianity   119
   The Writings and Canon   124

7. Canon as Prolegomenon for Theology   130

   Biblical or Canonical Theology   131
   The Jewish-Christian Connection   133
   Which Canon?   135
   Canonical Hermeneutics Revisited   137
      Problems and Task   139
      Structure   140
      Implications for Current Issues   143
      Interrelationship with Other Methods   145

   Toward the Future   146

Notes   149
Ancient Sources   157
Authors   161
Subjects   163

Preface

Research and thinking for this book began a decade ago at Cambridge University where a former teacher, Brevard Childs, was then finishing his Old Testament introduction. His lectures and private conversations interested me in the study of canon and its significance for my teaching and writing. That Childs was concerned to speak of the whole Bible as it functioned and functions within a community of faith was most important; such a perspective is critical for my context as a seminary teacher.

The most amorphous of canonical divisions in the Hebrew Bible—the Writings—quickly drew my attention. Parallels between Torah and the Gospels, between Prophets and the Apostles (Epistles) have been drawn since the second century B.C.E. I was struck, however, by the difficulty of finding parallels between the Writings as a canonical division and later Jewish and Christian literature. Subsequent research led me into pseudepigraphal literature and rabbinic literature, to search for explanations or a key to the Writings and their functions in the post-exilic period and beyond. This book is the result of that research. Although other explanations of the role and function of the Writings as canon might be made, this literature, I believe, addresses some pressing issues in biblical interpretation and biblical theology. Specifically, this often-neglected literature, viewed from the perspective of canon, has much to tell us about what it meant and means to be a biblical community and provides guidelines for future ecumenical and interfaith discussions. This study only begins to deal with some of these topics. My hope, however, is that further studies of this rich and enigmatic literature will continue.

Two other factors influenced my research. First, I became involved in one part of Jewish-Christian dialogue. The opportunity to study with scholars such as David Hartman and Paul van Buren convinced me that the post-exilic literature of Israel and the accompanying development of Jewish scriptures were essential for understanding the role of the Bible today. Immersion in the Talmud with Jews and Christians strengthened my conviction. Second, my own Episcopal church involved me in a series of Bible studies that resulted in the formation of many "new" communities. This too confirmed my belief that the Writings represent exactly this: communities formed and shaped in response to an authoritative body of texts.

This study is best seen as an essay about biblical interpretation. I would never have been able to write it without the pioneering work of Brevard Childs, James A. Sanders, and many others. At the same time, much in this study is new. The Writings are not an easy body of literature to categorize from a holistic and canonical perspective. The footnotes will enable others to continue such study, but there are no other full-scale treatments of the Writings as canon to which I can refer the reader.

To all those I have had the occasion to study with and learn from in this endeavor, I owe many thanks. James A. Sanders, Joseph Blenkinsopp, and John Barton read a "first" attempt at trying to make sense of the Writings. The present study, different from my first manuscript, is richer for their valuable suggestions. I must also thank Brevard Childs and my own students, all of whom have been in dialogue with me about canon and its function. John A. Hollar and the editorial staff, especially Timothy G. Staveteig, of Fortress Press have been patient through many delays and have provided invaluable suggestions about the ultimate shape of this study. Margo Delaney and Peggy Lester spent many hours typing and retyping various forms of this manuscript. Without them, especially Peggy Lester, I could not have finished.

Finally, I must thank, however inadequately, my wife, Alda Marsh Morgan. Not only did she read this entire manuscript and make many important suggestions for more felicitous ways to express myself but also she was a constant source of support and encouragement. From Alda I have learned more about what it means to be a member of a community with a biblical faith at its center than anyone else. It is to her that this book is dedicated.

D. F. Morgan

1

A Canonical View
of the Writings

PURPOSE AND CONTEXT

The purpose of this study is to present a description and analysis of the textual hermeneutics operative in the post-exilic times of ancient Israel and to trace their development into the early rabbinic and Christian period. It will be argued that the process of textual interpretation that produced the third part of the Hebrew canon, the Writings, provided normative paradigms for subsequent generations of Christians and Jews. Moreover, a study of the pertinent literature may aid in identifying more clearly the morphology of a "canonical" community.

This study maintains that the hermeneutics found in the Writings and continued into the Rabbinic and early Christian period are important for contemporary Christianity and Judaism as they seek to understand both their differences and their commonality. There will be no attempt to erase the differences between Judaism and Christianity in their divergent textual and confessional traditions. Indeed, it is precisely the collection and canonization of the diverse, sometimes even antithetical, literature in the Writings that provide both warrant for and explanation of the different expressions of faith that bind us and divide us. They bind us because the hermeneutics of post-exilic Israel share a response to a common, emerging scripture. They divide us because these hermeneutics also allow for the newness of our particular experiences to become normative and to move us in different directions. This study, then, is addressed to both Christians and Jews, for we are all shaped in part by the hermeneutics operative in the Writings.

Why the Writings? It is important to acknowledge how unimportant, relatively speaking, this literature has been for biblical theologians and, indeed, for contemporary faith communities. (The Writings consist of the Psalms, Job, Proverbs, Ecclesiastes, Ruth, Lamentations, Esther, the Song of Solomon, Ezra, Nehemiah, Daniel, and 1—2 Chronicles.) With the exception of the Psalms, this literature is not read regularly in the weekly liturgy, although the Megilloth (Ruth, Lamentations, Ecclesiastes, Esther, and the Song of Solomon) are read on special Jewish holy days. Rather, Torah and the Prophets, the Gospels, and the Epistles of St. Paul are the centerpieces of our scripture, at least as reflected in worship.

If we turn to biblical theology, much the same observation can be made. The great events (e.g., the Exodus, Sinai), heroes (e.g., the patriarchs, Moses, David), or theological topics (e.g., covenant, creation, salvation history) often receive the most attention, with the primary texts being Torah, Prophets, Gospels, and the Epistles. Although the place and role of wisdom and apocalyptic literature have enjoyed much attention in current biblical scholarship, there has been no suggestion that these important parts of the biblical message should become the center of a biblical theology.

There are some good reasons for this relative invisibility of the Writings. Historically, we know very little about the post-exilic period or the groups responsible for this literature's composition or collection. However, the same observation could be made for the patriarchal or Mosaic periods, the events, heroes, and theological topics of Torah, Prophets, the Gospels, and the Epistles that have been and continue to be central to Judaism and Christianity. In one sense the Writings are referential in nature, with their value being seen in terms of how well they do, or do not, make the Torah and Prophets relevant to their biblical communities. As we shall see, however, this referential nature of the Writings is an important dimension of the hermeneutics of biblical communities, past, present, and future. Although invisibility may thus be seen as one indication of how well the communities that produced the Writings have done their job, we must consciously and carefully study them if we are to follow responsibly their paths of interpretation. In many ways contemporary Jews and Christians find themselves in the same situation as the authors of the Writings, challenged to relate the scripture to the problems and needs of the present day.

If there are good and legitimate reasons for overlooking the Writings, there are also damaging consequences, especially for Christians. The post-exilic period (and its literature), sometimes referred to as the dark ages of Israel, is often a convenient place to locate the negative developments of Judaism (e.g., legalism, pariah communities) to which Jesus and the early church represent the Renaissance or Enlightenment. When all of the literature contained in the Writings is studied, accepting such summary judgments of Judaism in this period is difficult. As a whole the Writings reflect a multifaceted and pluralistic response by many different Jewish communities that cannot be easily or fairly characterized as "legalistic," "prophetic," or by any other one designation. Rather, in continuity with their predecessors, these communities and the literature they produced represent a wide variety of ways to be the people of God, bequeathing to later Jewish and Christian communities both the challenge and the necessity to follow in their stead.

The Writings are then, both in ancient and contemporary communities, partially invisible. They do not intend to present the definitive statements about the central events, heroes, or theological topics of the biblical tradition. For this reason biblical theologians have either neglected them or, worse yet, sometimes used them as scapegoats or stereotypes of the character of early Judaism. Such usage of this literature, its authors, and communities is unfortunate because the Writings, when viewed as a whole, represent hermeneutical responses to an emerging textual tradition. These responses testify both to the important normative force of those central texts and to the creative way in which the Writings shape our future response as biblical communities.

In order to achieve the goal of defining biblical interpretation in the post-exilic period, we will focus our attention on the Writings as a whole. In one sense, such a perspective is anachronistic, for this literature was surely not viewed as a canonical division until late in the post-exilic period. In another sense, however, the Writings are all post-exilic responses to an emerging scripture (Torah and Prophets), regardless of the provenance of individual proverbs, psalms, and so forth. The Writings in their entirety thus provide a literary and theological perspective that can be centered in a particular period. No claim is made here that other biblical literature (e.g., post-exilic prophecy) cannot also provide insight into the hermeneutics of post-exilic Israel. No other literature, however, has been purposely collected and juxtaposed to scripture in the same way as the Writings. Moreover, the interpretive paradigms found in this literature are capable of being traced into subsequent "writings." What the Writings demonstrate— a dynamic interpretation of texts within many different and diverse communities—continued. The canonization of this literature makes

such diverse interpretation normative for all future biblical communities. Therefore, an examination of the historical context of the Writings, of the theological paradigms represented, of the consequences
of making all of this literature a part of the canon in one division, of
the continuity with later "writings"—an examination of all of this is
valuable for understanding the place of Scripture and canon in early
Judaism and Christianity and in the present day.

This study falls into the category of biblical theology. Different ways
of imaging and describing God and community are at the heart of this
study. Although the hermeneutical paradigms we will present are de-
rived from an attempt to describe biblical literature, nevertheless, such
paradigms and the dynamic that produced them provide important
clues for the constructive task—the organization and development of
future biblical theologies. This study is motivated by and dependent
upon the creative ferment found in many current presentations of
biblical theology. A focus on history, on sociology, on the nature of
biblical literature—all of these are essential complements to my present work. The recent works of Hanson, Terrien, Westermann, Childs,
Sanders, Barr, and others provide important historical, sociological,
and theological insight that must be integrated into the hermeneutical
proposal made here. Although the holistic view of the Writings here
presented sheds, I hope, some light on the future tasks of biblical
theology as explicated by these scholars, many different perspectives
and proposals are needed to continue this work.

Finally, this study shares with its contemporary counterparts a concern over the "crisis" in biblical interpretation and the lack of a consensus about what is central to the task of writing a biblical theology.
Although we will need to distinguish the perspectives and position of
this work from those of James A. Sanders and Brevard Childs, it will
be claimed throughout this book that the concept of canon, as both
an interpretive context and a normative guide, is one way of ap-
proaching the theology of ancient Israel that has a chance to resolve
some of the problems currently probed by biblical theologians.[1] Such
a claim takes seriously the nature and function of the literature as
written, interpreted, and lived out in biblical communities both past
and present. Canon studies must surely recognize and utilize other
perspectives found within and without the biblical texts. However, to
dismiss the value of canon for biblical theology is, in my view, to fail
to see and understand an essential part of the biblical message and its
theological rationale.

THE WRITINGS AND CANONICAL
INTERPRETATION

It is generally agreed that the events and developments in the Judean exile and the early post-exilic period resulted in a community with the "Torah" at its center. Shortly thereafter the collection of literature associated with the "Prophets" also became an important part of the sacred texts of early Judaism. Speaking of "canon" at this time is perhaps anachronistic, for there is evidence that additions and adjustments to these basic texts were still being made. Nevertheless, this does not negate the fact that one of the most important, if not the most important, developments in early Judaism was the emergence of Torah and Prophets as scripture.

The beginning of such a process lies deep within the early history of Israel and has been traced admirably by Noth, von Rad, and others. However, to begin to speak of Torah or Prophets as fairly stable collections of scripture that are central to the life of all subsequent Jewish communities is possible only in the post-exilic period. In such a historical and literary context, the Writings and the communities that produced them become significant. The Writings, the roots of which are also to be found in the pre-exilic period, are best understood as responses of communities with Torah and Prophets as their central textual tradition. This literature is the product of sages, scribes, singers, prayers, community builders, visionaries, and storytellers. It represents a discussion among those writers, their communities, and the foundational texts of early Judaism. As we shall see, such a dialogue was often complex because an ever-present tension between Torah and Prophets made their proper use and interpretation subject to debate. Added to this were the continual new challenges brought to the different communities in the post-exilic period by the changing circumstances in which they lived. As a result, the dialogue between text and community represented by the Writings inevitably produced different approaches to scripture, different visions of social structure, and different conceptions of who God is and what the people were called to be. The literature of the Writings will not, therefore, provide us with unitary conceptions of God, scripture, or community. Rather, taken as a whole, as a collection of diverse literature, the Writings will constantly point us toward dialogue between text and community. Surely that dialogue was always a critical part of Israel's history. Indeed, when Torah and Prophets as a definable if not totally stable Scripture become the "text," the Writings initiate a hermeneutical process that continues to be central, even normative, for the life of future biblical communities.[2]

In order to study the Writings in this way, we need to engage in contemporary biblical theology. Two examples will suffice: pluralism and diversity. The Writings, viewed historically and theologically, reflect at least three different types of pluralism. Explaining the divergent perspectives found in this literature is impossible without presupposing a cultural pluralism. With the Diaspora, Judaism would forever be found in many different cultures. The Writings represent the differing attempts of several communities separated by time, space, and culture to respond to Torah and Prophets.

In addition to cultural pluralism, we also need to recognize a scriptural pluralism. The message of Torah and Prophets is not homogeneous or monolithic. It contains many different ways to resolve issues of community identity and mission. The authors of the Writings, although responding to a common textual tradition, are confronted by the rich diversity within it. Even without a cultural pluralism, it would be surprising, if not impossible, were the communities of the post-exilic period to respond to Torah and Prophets in the same way. The Writings confirm this judgment.

Finally, we may speak of canonical pluralism. Although such a phenomenon does not become operative until after Tanak (Torah, Prophets, and Writings) is finally accepted as canon, keeping this type of pluralism in mind is important from the outset of our study. It is arguable that both cultural and scriptural pluralism are merely ideological constructs, probably based on our own contemporary conceptions of religion and society. That is, although cultural and scriptural pluralism have value in helping us to structure and explain the differences found in post-exilic Israel's literature and in Torah and Prophets, in fact, none of the communities represented is necessarily pluralistic in nature. To cite the most obvious example, characterizing the perspectives of Ezra and Nehemiah as pluralistic is difficult. When the Writings are viewed holistically, however, when Ezra-Nehemiah is juxtaposed to Ruth and other post-exilic literature, then we may surely speak of pluralism. This canonical pluralism is a heritage of differing perspectives concerning God and community that are the property of all and must be taken seriously by all.

The problem of diversity has always been a central issue for biblical theology. Indeed, the literature of the Writings is a prime example of the diversity in the Bible and has often created problems for those who wish to impose a theological system upon it. Where do we put "wisdom literature"? How do we explain the different community identities represented by the books of Ezra and Daniel, and can they possibly fit within one theological system? Certainly descriptions of the interrelationship of these different books and their communities can and have been accomplished through a study of history and tradition, but such approaches have often been eschewed by biblical theologians for their failure to find an appropriate and workable theological system into which all of the diversity can be "fit."[3] The longstanding debate over whether such attempts are "histories of religion" or "biblical theologies" is but one of the ways in which the difficulty of this task is expressed. Here I argue that diversity, as represented in the Writings viewed as a whole, is a positive component of biblical theology rather than an irritant for those who seek a system based on a clear and homogeneous theological definition of God, Israel, covenant, or the like. The common denominator would appear not to be any particular definition, theological or otherwise, but rather the dialogue between text (Torah and Prophets) and community. It is that dialogue that has been canonized. It is that dialogue that has become critical to the definition of what it means to be a scriptural and a canonical community. It is that dialogue, as reflected in the Writings and subsequent Christian and Jewish literature, that must be taken seriously by biblical theologians. In one sense, the Writings systematize diversity and make it forever a characteristic of later biblical communities. The implications of such a view are great for late-twentieth-century biblical theologies.

To study the Writings from a canonical perspective is a twofold task. Although we begin with a literature that has its definition, delimitation, and theological function within the Hebrew Bible as a canonical division, if we are to understand the richness of the textual dialogue found in it, then we must approach this literature first as the product of post-exilic communities. History, theology, and canon are intertwined. We cannot ignore the groups who produced this literature and the needs they sought to meet if we are to explain adequately the dialogue between community and text to which they testify.

At the same time, to focus on the Writings as canon is to go beyond the particular interests and motives of its authors and its communities. To engage in canonical hermeneutics is to become enmeshed in a textual dynamic that, although it rests upon the struggles of particular groups, is now operating at a different level. On this level, for example, the historical particularity of the literature is erased. It no longer matters what Ezra intended to do, but rather how we are to relate the

Ezra literature to Ruth, Esther, and Daniel. In this sense each of the Writings becomes one—but only one—way of responding to and of reading scripture within the larger canonical section of which it is a part. The Writings, viewed canonically, must be read historically to bring out the richness and the diversity of each book. Ultimately, however, they need to be read as a whole if the hermeneutical patterns and paradigms they represent are to be seen as functional for later communities.

I maintain that the dialogue represented in the Writings continues into early rabbinic Judaism and Christianity. Such a position is dependent not simply or primarily upon a notion of historical development, upon a "natural" dialogue between text and community that is always characteristic of a biblical community. Rather, it is the interpretive patterns found in the Writings, which are then canonized and made normative for subsequent communities, that best explain both the continuity and the discontinuity between later Judaism and Christianity. For this reason, tracing some of these later literary developments is important in order to demonstrate the value and import of the canonical hermeneutics, which begin but are not finished in the Writings. These hermeneutics are constitutive not only for Tanak but also for Talmud and the New Testament.

STRUCTURE AND FORMAT

In order to place the methods and perspectives of this study within the contemporary discussion of biblical theology, some attention must be given to recent discussions of canon interpretation and theology. Thus chapter 2 presents a fuller description of canonical hermeneutics, epitomized in the work of Brevard Childs and James A. Sanders. I do not wish to rehearse the history of "canonical criticism" or to review the many important works of these authors and others. Rather, through an examination of the ways in which canon can be seen to be an important concept for biblical theology, I will address the primary issues involved for interpreting the Writings. In doing so, a way of examining the Writings from a canonical perspective will be set forth that is neither that of Childs nor that of Sanders, although I am indebted to both.

Chapters 3 and 4 are the heart of this study. Chapter 3 first presents a brief overview of the post-exilic period and a discussion of the central authoritative texts, Torah and Prophets, to which the communities of the post-exilic period responded. The remainder of the chapter focuses on the particular needs and agendas of post-exilic Israel as reflected in the Writings. Special attention is given to the literary ways in which these writers expressed themselves. Chapter 4 then focuses on the ways in which the authoritative texts of Torah and Prophets are actually used and on the resultant literary and theological paradigms that are produced. These interpretive paradigms are reflective both of the communities of post-exilic Israel and of the texts to which they respond. Community shapes text (chapter 3), and text shapes community (chapter 4).

Chapter 5 traces the continuity of the interpretive paradigms found in the Writings in the subsequent literature of Judaism and Christianity. Attention is focused chiefly on the texts; an analysis of the communities in this period lies beyond my purview. It is hoped, however, that this later literature surveyed, compared, and contrasted with the hermeneutical patterns found in the Writings will recover and affirm the ongoing dialogue initiated by the post-exilic literature.

Chapter 6 addresses the consequences of the Writings becoming canon. The stability of the hermeneutical pattern thus achieved and affirmed by later canonical literature is discussed.

Finally, chapter 7 examines the implications of this study for biblical or canonical theology in the future. It suggests that canonical interpretation, especially as found in the Writings and continued in the later literature of both Judaism and Christianity, provides some guidelines for those who wish to study and describe the structure and the central issues of the theology of the Bible. Although canon is not the panacea for all problems, it does partially explain "why we are where we are" and perhaps where we may be able to go in the future.

The goals of this study are clear. Through a study of the historical development of the Writings in the post-exilic period of Israel, we seek to describe the scriptural hermeneutics that have become a part of the canon and foundational for future Jews and Christians. A dialogue, or rather many dialogues, between community and text is essential for these hermeneutics. The resultant pattern, canonized, is critical for Christians and Jews, regardless of the canon that is central to each. What the Writings represent can be seen as a major characteristic of all subsequent biblical communities and canons—the latter are variations that prove the point.

Finally, an observation about the history of Judaism and Christianity is now in order. It has often been noted that a critical difference between these two religions is the centrality of Torah for the former and the centrality of Christ for the latter. Recently, however, some scholars have argued that such a characterization of Judaism is inaccurate, that the sage and the "Oral Torah" are much more the center of rabbinic Judaism. If this is indeed the case, then in both Judaism and Christianity we must see a hermeneutical process that values later developments as pivotal to the definition of both religious traditions. Such an observation would appear to be affirmed by the canons of both Judaism (Tanak-Talmud) and Christianity (Old Testament–New Testament). At first glance, such an observation might also appear to reverse the hermeneutics, the referential quality, of the Writings as they relate to Torah and Prophets. However, what the Writings represent is several different communities trying to do to a greater or lesser degree exactly what later Judaism and Christianity have done: to read their scripture in light of the normative lens of their own visions, hopes, and new revelations. In one sense the Writings fail, for it is later revelations and literature that provide the hermeneutical paradigms and become normative. In a deeper and more important sense they succeed, for they provide the warrant, and in some cases the paradigms, for Jesus, the apostles, the rabbis, and contemporary Jews and Christians.

2

Canon and Interpretation

What difference does it make to study biblical literature from a canonical perspective? What issues, principles, and presuppositions are involved? Does such an endeavor rely upon particular and new methodologies for the interpretation of the text? How is canonical study related to other more traditional methods such as form criticism and literary criticism? These and other questions are raised by this study and many others, which argue that canon represents an important element in the overall interpretation of the biblical message. The purpose of this chapter is to provide an interpretive framework, based on an understanding of the biblical canon and its function, from which the writings may be viewed in a holistic, focused, and circumscribed way. Giving special attention to interpretation of the Writings as canon, both the necessary presuppositions and the methodological guidelines that direct or control such a study of this literature are explored. Finally, a canonical hermeneutic applied to the Writings is described.

CANONICAL CRITICISM

The origins of recent canon studies, epitomized in the work of Brevard Childs and James A. Sanders, are diverse and complex.[1] On the one hand, they represent a continuation of older, long-standing concerns within biblical scholarship. The hermeneutical problems raised by historical criticism—for example, getting from what the text "meant" to what it "means"—are one of the motivations for canonical studies. As such, advocates of canonical hermeneutics find themselves in the company of Karl Barth and Rudolf Bultmann, who addressed similar problems, albeit with different solutions proposed. Even the suggestion of a "new" approach to biblical theology, a new hermeneutical principle, is itself not new but represents a continuing activity within biblical scholarship.

On the other hand, the concern to place canon in the center of biblical interpretation is motivated by at least two new phenomena affecting biblical studies of the past generation. First, recently discovered texts at Qumran and elsewhere have raised serious questions about the shape and role of canon. Sanders's earliest writing on the Qumran Psalter collections reflects in part the stimulus these ancient textual witnesses have provided for his subsequently developed "canonical criticism."[2] Second, all of biblical scholarship has been influenced by the increasing importance given to pluralism in contemporary society. The breakdown of religious and cultural consensus, and the search for new identity and integrity by previously oppressed or subordinated groups—this process has had an impact upon every aspect of biblical interpretation. In this regard, we may see the recent focus on canon as representative of a desire both to present and justify diversity and to find a basis for a common ground, if not a consensus, for dialogue and biblical interpretation. How successful such attempts will be in solving old problems and addressing new ones remains to be seen.

Although the origins and motivation for canon studies are difficult to determine with precision, nevertheless there appears to be some agreement about the goals of such work. Canon should be a central datum for biblical interpretation and theology. The need of the contemporary community of faith to focus on an authoritative text and to reflect theologically upon it is at the heart of contemporary canonical analysis. Such general goals and the affirmation of the importance of canon do not take us very far, however, because the analyses produced by canon critics differ dramatically. Precisely at this point serious problems of method, definition, and direction are raised. Not only are the motivations, if not the overall goals, of Childs, Sanders, and others different, so also are their basic starting points and their methods. A survey of canon studies reveals a great deal of confusion about *how* to study the Bible as canon.[3] Therefore, it is necessary to discuss the methods of canonical study here, even though such an endeavor is threatened by the Scylla of Childs, the Charybdis of Sanders, and a host of other biblical scholars who either chart many different courses between them or abandon the attempt altogether. This observation should not be viewed as a deterrent for proceeding, for canon studies have much to offer the discipline of biblical theology and the contemporary faith community. However, great care must be exercised in determining the methods appropriate for viewing the Writings as canon.

Fundamental to the study of canon and interpretation is the distinct relationship between community and text. This relationship has been described as a "dynamic," a "dialectic," or a "dialogue." We prefer to use the term *dialogue*, because "dynamic" appears to characterize an aspect of the interrelationship rather than defining the interrelationship itself, and "dialectic" presupposes a particular process and result, which may or may not occur.

To discuss community and text raises other important questions. *Which* text? *Which* community? A study of the canon is ultimately concerned with the text which is authoritative within the contemporary community of faith. At the same time, to understand the nature of that text and its possible functions today, we must study earlier forms of the text and the nature of the ancient communities that used them. Therefore, the task of constructing an interpretation of the Writings based on canon is twofold: (1) to study the interrelationship of ancient community and text; and (2) to present a constructive proposal that accounts for the means by which that interrelationship has continued into the present.

The danger inherent in any approach to canon is to focus too much attention on either text or community. On the one hand, the text neither does in fact nor can in possibility function without a community. On the other hand, the community, either ancient or contemporary, cannot simply decide what its "text" means without giving serious attention to the text's structure, function, and intent. Although Childs and Sanders among others recognize and affirm these as true, the former is most interested in the canonical text and the latter focuses largely on the canonical community. I will attempt to highlight the text-community dialogue so essential to canon without choosing either community or text as primary. Questions of canonical method and perspective must be answered by giving full attention to both parts of this dialogue. The picture of canon and interpretation that emerges is in part a conflation of Childs and Sanders, perhaps unacceptable to either, but, I hope, pertinent and valuable for understanding the Writings and the subsequent canonical literature of Christians and Jews.

CANON AND AUTHORITY

Fundamental to the nature of canon is the question of authority. The function of canon is normative for the text-community dialogue it reflects. Although students of canon interpretation generally affirm an authoritative and normative function for canon, they often focus on either the textual or communal nature of that authority.

Over and over again, Brevard Childs refers to canon as the authoritative form of the Scriptures as received and transmitted by the community of faith. Such a view is not simply applied to the biblical text and times, for "Scripture is normative for the obedient life of the church."[4] Although such a position can be justified by reference to the varieties of ways in which communities of faith have used and described the text authoritatively, Childs is primarily concerned with the theological norms embedded in the text itself. All of his canonical analyses of biblical texts intend to provide theological perspectives and structures that are authoritative for the community in whatever context the community finds itself. For Childs, to find the normativeness of Scripture one does not search for a process within the community reflected in the text. Rather, the overall structure of a book (e.g., Genesis, Isaiah, Mark) provides a theological construct that is normative for the community, regardless of who wrote it, when it was written, or what prompted its being written. Surely we must also relate the different theological messages found in scriptural books to one another in our effort to find an overall biblical and authoritative message for ancient or contemporary communities. For Childs, however, such a process is not dependent upon historical reconstruction or special attention to particular biblical communities and their needs.[5]

For Sanders, however, the authority of canon is closely tied to the needs and crises of particular communities of faith. Indeed, the issue of authority itself arises in periods of the history of Israel when questions of identity and survival were central. The very shape of canon is reflected in the answers to these questions. To speak, as Sanders does, of the canon as stable and adaptable, as life-giving in quality, as pluralistic, as answering the question of identity, is to focus on the community side of the canon dialogue.[6]

It would be unfair to suggest that Sanders, Childs, and others are not concerned with both community and text when they discuss the authority of canon. My purpose is to make clear what is primary for each: Childs emphasizes the textual side of the normative dialogue; Sanders, by focusing on the questions of how and why the text is normative, highlights the community's role in this dialogical process.

For the purposes of this study, to recognize the authoritative nature of canon for the Writings means we must first affirm the existence of a textual tradition that was normative for post-exilic Israel. In chapters 3 and 4 we will attempt to identify the nature and shape of those normative texts, Torah and Prophets. Sometimes the Writings witness to the authority of the text through direct reference to it; at other times the authority of the text is more oblique. In any case, to analyze the Writings from a canonical perspective is to posit an authoritative text that provided normative direction.

A canonical view of the Writings must also address the community side of the dialogue by asking how the text was used authoritatively. We must examine the needs of particular communities that sought to use authoritative texts to resolve issues of community identity, social organization, and mission. This was often accomplished through the creation of new texts that presented the nature and will of God for ancient Israel. Nevertheless, such interpretations are grounded in the use of an authoritative text by particular communities for particular purposes.

Finally, the relationship of the structure and function of the Writings as a whole to the question of authority must be briefly addressed. For some, canonical structure, theologically conceived, is authoritative. For others, the question of function is primary: Structure follows function. Once again, an emphasis on the text or the community often results in these different assessments. When examining the Writings as a whole, with many different canonical orders of the books and with their diverse content, assuming that structure is not important would be easy. What if, however, the potpourri nature of the Writings and their ultimate dispersion to many different places within the Christian canon were seen as reflective of their function? Then, diversity and adaptability would be central to their authority. The implications of such a notion of authority are great for biblical theology and must be explored.

COMMUNITY AND TEXT IN DIALOGUE

To speak of canon is to speak of text and community in dialogue. In the process of this dialogue, the text is shaped by the community and its particular needs. The community is also shaped by the text and its story, its values. The implications of such observations vary depending upon whether or not the text is already perceived to be canon, that is, to be fixed and unchangeable. In the early post-exilic period this was surely not the case. Additions and corrections could be made to Torah and Prophets, and other writings could be produced, all of which could become a part of the scriptural canon. During this period the content and structure of the text are literally being shaped by the community; at the same time the social structure, identity, and mission of the community are being shaped by a growing authoritative textual corpus.

In later periods, when no more "writings" are capable of being added to the biblical canon, the shaping of the text by the community is accomplished by the way in which it is read and interpreted. We may perhaps speak of a "canon within a canon" at this point. Communities select those parts of the canon that they will use to understand, even to justify, the way they will live out the authoritative story. Although we agree that the canon as a whole remains authoritative for the community, nonetheless, no community can structure its concept of mission, identity, and social norms without highlighting some scripture and often ignoring or disagreeing with other scripture. In all of this, the community-shaping function of canon remains constant, regardless of the changing or unchanging nature of the text.

To begin to study canon, recognizing the dialogue upon which it rests, one needs to decide whether to focus on the text (scripture) or the process (community) that produced it. Although both text and process as foci have their source in the biblical text itself, selecting an entry point is still necessary. We choose to begin with the community side of the dialogue. The rationale for this starting point rests on a basic hermeneutical observation: Texts are authoritative, referred to, and used because of concerns within the contemporary community. Interpretation begins with the community and its reasons for viewing a text as authoritative.

Community

Sanders focuses upon community process when discussing the nature and function of canon. Accepting the centrality of Torah for exilic and post-exilic Israel, he suggests that the shapers of this authoritative text were faced with existential questions of identity and survival caused by the catastrophes associated with the fall of Judah. The resultant text was shaped by the realities of a lost monarchy and state and by the needs to define community in light of these events.[7] Some have reacted negatively to this "existentialist" approach and suggested that the functions and message of canon cannot be equated merely with questions about identity or the exilic experience.[8] To the extent that we wish only to analogize from the historical situation of ancient Israel in order to understand the function and message of canon in the contemporary faith community, such negative reactions are in order. Surely the message and use of canon today should not be dependent

solely upon how an earlier community viewed its problems. The canon
is far too multivalent in its functions, use, and message for this. Any
discussion of canon, however, also needs to include the communal
process that used it. We are heirs both of the text and of the transmission and shaping process that produced it. Whether Torah is a
product of the exilic community may or may not be a critically important problem to solve. What is important is that the Torah was
shaped by a community seeking to understand its relationship to the
authoritative tradition of the past in light of particular problems and
challenges. This is a fundamental assumption for canon studies and
necessitates study of the community.

Text

Childs begins his study of canon with the received text of the canon
in its final form, as do all canonical critics. This authoritative final form
shapes subsequent biblical communities. Clearly Childs refers here to
a time when canon has become a fixed form.[9] Little time is spent trying
to outline in detail the communal process that produced the final text
because authority is found in the textual form that resulted from such
a process, rather than in the process itself. Nevertheless, Childs and
others do study the compositional histories of biblical books that are
indeed reflective of a process, communal in nature, that produced the
final form. However, Childs deliberately eschews any attempt to locate
such textual shaping in a special community with its particular needs
and concerns. The text transcends the communities that produced it
and represents an authoritative message for all who receive the text.
With the text in its final form as a starting point, the student of canonical
form must search for the theological construal of the text. Once such
a construal has been achieved, the "intertextuality" of the Bible must
be taken seriously as we seek to relate the message of one book to
another.[10] Such a way of reading would prevent the phenomenon of
"a canon within a canon," in theory if not in practice.

There are, then, two consequences of viewing canon as a dialogue
between text and community for our study of the Writings and canonical hermeneutics. The Writings need to be set clearly and firmly
within the communities of post-exilic Israel if we are to understand
their function, and the final form of the Writings needs to be viewed
as a canonical division. Such a construal of the Writings is seemingly
anachronistic; many question whether such a canonical division was
operative in the post-exilic period. Yet, such a construal relativizes the
issue of history, that is, the post-exilic period of the composition of

the Writings. There is a tension between the final form and intent of the Writings as a whole and the historical communities that produced this literature. We seek not to erase this tension but to highlight it. Such a tension calls attention to the diversity of the particular communities responding to Torah and Prophets, while at the same time it demands that we relate this diversity to an authoritative structure accepted by later communities. The authority of canon and its structure is not to be found in a study of either the final textual form or the community, but in both, through the dialogue between them.

SCRIPTURE AND TORAH

Before proceeding, a few clarifications about the distinction between "canon" and "scripture" are in order. Moreover, because the hermeneutics represented in the Writings are dependent upon a dialogue that begins before the Writings themselves are completed, some attention should be given to the function and shape of Torah as it illustrates that dialogue and mandates its continuance in the Writings.

In the early post-exilic period, to speak of "canon" as a fixed, unchangeable, and final collection of Scripture is inappropriate. There is no clear evidence that the canon of Hebrew scripture was organized and referred to as Torah, Prophets, and Writings until well into the Common Era. It is, of course, possible to escape this problem by refusing to speak clearly about the historical setting and intentions of the particular communities that produced "Torah," "Prophets," or "Writings." Yet anyone who would study the literature of ancient Israel from a canonical perspective must also recognize the time-conditioned nature of that literature and the communities that produced it. The fact that this literature is perceived as a canonical collection only at a later time must be taken into account. This is true for our study of the Writings at two different levels.

First, and to repeat, the Writings as a collected body of scripture are not canon in the early post-exilic period. There is evidence (e.g., the Prologue to Ecclesiasticus) that some of this literature was seen as a third part of the sacred texts of Judaism by the second century B.C.E. At the same time, there is no indication that the "Writings" were the common property of all Jewish communities. Indeed, one of the books, Daniel, was probably not written until very late in this period, much less a part of a larger whole called the Writings. To use canon as a way of organizing our study of this literature, prior to its final

collection into a third division, is therefore to be involved in a constructive task. This task is indicated and necessitated by our contemporary concerns rather than by the texts as written in the post-exilic
period. Such a perspective is critical for understanding the present
function and shape of this literature.

Second, a historical focus on community and text must also recognize that even Torah and Prophets were not canon in the sense of
completed literature in this period. Changes and additions were still
being made to this literature. Nevertheless, Torah and Prophets were
authoritative post-exilic texts to which the Writings were related and
to which they responded. Here the distinction between *scripture*, as
authoritative text still capable of being changed and adapted, and
canon, as a fixed and final collection of *Scripture*, becomes pertinent.
In order to avoid the criticism of projecting an anachronistic view of
canon into the post-exilic period, the term scripture will be used to
refer to Torah and Prophets at this time, in whatever forms they take.
That there were such collected textual traditions in the post-exilic
period that functioned as scripture is not debated. Further, although
surely some of the literature of the Writings may have already begun
to have a scriptural status itself (e.g., Psalms), we maintain this status
was always secondary to that of Torah and Prophets, always in need
of being related to these primary literary corpora for their authority
and point of reference.

Canonical hermeneutics, in this study, is concerned with the interaction between these precanonical authoritative scriptures (Torah and
Prophets) and the post-exilic communities which responded to them
in the literature they produced and collected, which ultimately became
the Writings. Although the dialogue between Torah-Prophets (text)
and Writings (community) does not become canonical itself until a
later period, the primary components of that dialogue are set much
earlier.

Thus, to study the canonical hermeneutics of the post-exilic period
requires that we refer to both "scripture" and "canon." Because these
hermeneutics presuppose a dialogue between authoritative texts and
a community that perceives and uses them as such, we refer to such
texts as "scripture." Because, however, the shape and nature of that
dialogue are best illustrated by viewing the literature contained in the
Writings viewed as a whole, we use "canon" as a constructive and
heuristic device to identify and organize that literature. Canons come
and go—they change from one community to another. Surely this is
well illustrated by the histories of Christianity and Judaism. The thesis

of this study, however, is that the hermeneutics represented by the Writings are a basic part of the continuing canonical histories of both Judaism and Christianity, regardless of the different canons found in each community. Indeed, such hermeneutics help to explain why the communities did what they did. For this reason, canon, with all of its problems, in its time-conditioned and community-specific nature, is an essential ingredient for a constructive approach to the Writings and to contemporary biblical theology.

In describing the nature of canon and canonical hermeneutics, we are invariably drawn into a variety of polarities. These polarities are often used to describe the nature of canon (e.g., adaptability-stability), the theological task as it relates to canon (e.g., descriptive-constructive), and the modes of canonical hermeneutics (e.g., prophetic-constitutive). All of these polarities or dichotomies arise in part from the central characteristic of canon and canonical hermeneutics: *the dialogue between community and authoritative text*. This observation may be illustrated by placing some of the typical polarities underneath the primary divisions of text and community.

Text	*Community*
Stability	Adaptability
Ethos	Mythos
Constitutive	Prophetic
Descriptive	Constructive
Stipulation	Story

Such a picture reflects the need for community and text to be included in any approach that takes canon seriously and asks how a text is to function authoritatively for the community of faith. The purpose of such a picture is not to suggest which "side" of the dialogue functions prophetically or constructively, for these may change. Rather, its purpose is to affirm that canon, as a conceptual and living entity, is neither text nor community only but both text and community in interrelationship. Although the impetus for canonical hermeneutics or interpretation begins with the needs of the community, in the new revelations and problems found there, the hermeneutics are not complete, or canonical, without the text becoming a central part of the dialogue.

The Writings themselves not only testify to such a dialogue but also provide paradigmatic and authoritative direction for the continuance of such a dialogical process within community. The Writings, however, do not begin such a dialogical process. We find it in the foundational and central text of Torah itself. All canonical critics have stressed the importance of Torah as canon for all subsequent Jewish and Christian communities. Many have also noted the critical functions that Deuteronomy, the last book of the Torah, possesses. Among its most important functions are: (1) the particular reinterpretation of the "law" found in this book; and (2) the fact that the inclusion of this book truncates the foundational story of ancient Israel, focusing not on the conquest and settlement of the promised land and the fulfillment of the promise to Abraham, but rather on the basic identity of the people with a book, the law of Moses.

Although both of these functions are important, we wish to examine briefly another aspect of Deuteronomy and its structural placement in the Pentateuch that is critical for understanding the nature of Torah as canon as well as the Writings. Childs has aptly noted: "It is, therefore, built into the canonical function of Deuteronomy that a new application of old tradition is being offered."[11] We would press this observation one step further: it is built into the canonical function of Torah that a new application of old tradition is being offered! That is, the function of Deuteronomy cannot be seen apart from the authoritative tradition (Genesis-Numbers) to which it is a response.[12] Moses, prophetic and authoritative figure par excellence, is reinterpreting the old story, applying new insights and values to the received tradition that will be essential when the people finally enter the promised land. However, the value of Moses in Deuteronomy for the structure of Torah as canon does not lie ultimately in the particular theological concerns found within this book. Rather, Moses as interpreter becomes an authoritative paradigm for all subsequent Torah communities. The story and stipulations can only be reinterpreted in light of changing circumstances. Moses did it; so must later scribes, sages, singers, community builders, and visionaries. Torah as a whole not only recognizes this need but also makes such a process normative for the future, whether in the "promised land" or not.

Text	Community
Story and Stipulation	Moses
Genesis-Numbers	Deuteronomy
Descriptive	Constructive

Viewed in this way, the structure of Torah may be related to the canonical polarities we have discussed above.

It has been suggested that canonization represents a process of sterilization in that the text is no longer an active, growing entity. One recent commentator has stated, "Canonization (even in its early, imperfect state) dried up the flow of direct information from God to man (or was it the other way around, that the drying up was responsible for the canonization?), forcing man to rely on Midrash, an intellectual endeavor that anchors the present in the past."[13] We suggest that such a picture is incongruent with the paradigmatic nature of the Torah, which mandates a continual and life-giving dialogue between the old and the new, between text and community. It is this dialogue, found already in Torah, that the Writings and later Christian and Jewish communities continue.

METHODOLOGICAL PRINCIPLES
AND GUIDELINES

Once the "text" and the "community" have been identified, how does an analysis of canonical hermeneutics proceed? What methods are peculiar to the study of canon? How are they to be related to other methods? Precisely at this crucial juncture in the study of canon the most debate occurs, with a resultant lack of clarity. Because canonical critics differ with regard to the primary object of their study, it is not surprising that their methodological approaches are different as well. Although many suggestions have been made regarding method, nevertheless, no clear guidelines by which everyone might be expected to achieve similar results have been provided. We will present the methodological perspectives that appear to have the most promise and importance for the study of the Writings and canon.

The relationship of a canonical approach to historical-critical methods is important. Because the intention and setting of the "author," however defined, is crucial to a historical approach, Childs is often seen as rejecting the value of such methods.[14] For him the intention and message of the canon transcends that of its "authors." Sanders, on the contrary, with his concern to trace a hermeneutical process historically, relies heavily upon historical methods. At the same time, the "canonical criticism" of Sanders also examines the way in which the canon has functioned after its composition. Although the history of the community remains important for such an endeavor, other methods, complementary to traditional historical ones, are needed.

All canonical critics, regardless of different starting points and regardless of their rhetoric that claims something "new" for a canonical approach, rely upon historical methods. For example, in determining the canonical structure of each biblical book, we are dependent upon the methods of form criticism, tradition-history, and redaction criticism. This is true even if we eschew and de-emphasize conclusions concerning the author's intention and the historical setting. These methods are used to determine genre definition and structure and to describe theological message and structure. Historical conclusions about author and intention can be important for obtaining a picture of historical process within community. Sanders sees the need to use critical methods in a particular sequence if we are to understand the final, canonical function of the text.[15] Once again, the emphasis upon canon as text or as community process is responsible for these different uses of historical method.

Interpretation of Community

One of the primary tasks of canonical hermeneutics is to study the way in which texts function authoritatively within the community. For the Writings in the post-exilic period, we must examine the various ways in which this literature uses Torah and Prophets. Such an examination requires a use of all the traditional historical methods in order to identify the texts referred to and their particular functions. In addition, however, we may also need to engage in "comparative midrash," which goes beyond the method of tradition-history by assuming a particular shape and development for the text and an authoritative function that is new for the post-exilic period.[16] In studying the canonical hermeneutics of the community, Sanders has proposed several "principles and rules" (context, covenant identity, memory, dynamic analogy, ambiguity of reality, mirrors for identity, theologizing and moralizing). Whether such rules and principles are ultimately helpful for our study of the Writings depends in large part on their ability to provide and illustrate a rationale for the use made of Torah and Prophets by the community, then and now. In our textual study, we seek to identify the "common" (old?) and "uncommon" (new?). This points to a fundamental characteristic of the text-community dialogue as the community seeks to relate the authoritative story to an equally authoritative set of new circumstances, challenges, and revelations of divine will.

Sanders has conceptualized the dynamics of canonical hermeneutics through a triangle composed of Tradition/Text, Sociological Context/ Situation, and Hermeneutics.[17] The hermeneutics section or "angle" of the triangle is critical for Sanders, for this is where the "rules and principles" and the modes of canonical hermeneutics are to be found. Never to be separated from text and context, and always subject to the "freedom of the grace of God," these hermeneutics are to be studied primarily through the methods of comparative midrash and tradition-history. The value of such a triangle and the resultant picture of canonical hermeneutics lies in its refusal to identify the "word" of God with either the text or the community. Nevertheless, as we have already seen, the way the community interpreted the function of the text is at the heart of the hermeneutical process and is capable of being traced historically. This does not represent the only perspective necessary for a canonical approach, but it is one vital ingredient in our study of the Writings.

Literary Context, Paradigm, Structure

If we must pay careful attention to the way in which post-exilic Israel used authoritative texts in our quest to understand canonical hermeneutics, then we must also recognize that the structure and shape of the Writings as a whole, indeed the canon as a whole, represent another dimension for our study and require other methodological perspectives. The "final form" of the text is an essential component in ascertaining the nature of the text's authority and function within the community. Therefore, the call to read the text "holistically" is important, with two possible foci for such a holistic reading of the canon distinguishable.

On the one hand, we may read a biblical book holistically. Childs has provided examples of such "readings" for every biblical book.[18] Although the theological insights gained from such an endeavor are great, several problems are also raised if we assume that such holistic reading was ever a common activity within either Christian or Jewish communities. Although we accept the thesis that "final form" was authoritative, it is not demonstrable that such a form required holistic reading. Indeed, the history of biblical interpretation would seem to indicate precisely the reverse, namely, the community read and interpreted particular verses, pericopes, or sections of a biblical book with no particular attention to any overall principle or message to be associated with a final form, theologically construed.[19]

On the other hand, a holistic reading of the canon can refer to the entirety of the texts (books) within it that must be taken into account when discussing canonical hermeneutics. This holistic construal of the canon is very important in our methodological approach to the Writings. Such a perspective need not assume or demand that any particular post-exilic community was cognizant of all other uses and functions of Torah and Prophets, only that the canon now demands *we* be aware of them. To put it another way, the normative nature of the Writings rests in part on a view that examines them as a whole, in all their diversity. In this sense we agree with Childs, who states that "attention to the diversity of the Old Testament witness does provide an initial critical norm within which to pursue theological reflection."[20]

The methods we may use to study the form of canon and in particular the Writings are somewhat different from those employed to determine the way in which a particular community viewed Torah and Prophets in the post-exilic period. One favorite term of Childs is "intertextuality," by which he refers to a dynamic and to patterns found within the whole canonical text. Such an approach is in part dependent upon form and redaction criticism, among other historical methods. To delineate the nature of this intertextuality, however, it is also clear that we may use other methods (e.g., structuralism, various forms of literary criticism) to determine these patterns and textual interrelationships. The appeal and value of these latter methods lie in their focus on the text and its particular functions without necessarily emphasizing "historical" communities, authors, and their intentions. The rules for such textual study are difficult to describe and often rest upon the special insights of the critics and their different notions of value and theology.[21] Nevertheless, the final form provides a common starting point. Childs, as Sanders, sees two modes for such a canonical approach: the descriptive and the constructive. Although Childs suggests that these modes represent options for the contemporary interpreter, there is no reason to believe such options were not functional for the ancient community as well. The community-text dialogue contains both the need to describe the authoritative traditions as well as to construct a theological message, and finally a canon, pertinent and applicable to the present life of the community.

This is precisely what the Writings represent and model for the contemporary faith community. In order to understand and explicate the canonical hermeneutics of this literature, we must first study the functions of these particular texts in post-exilic Israel. At the same time, we must pay special attention to the resultant shape of the literature produced, for this provides a major interpretive paradigm, or rather several paradigms, by which the text is brought to life. We should not suggest that this final shape of the Writings represented a consensus view for all post-exilic communities. Nor should we assume that the communities responsible for shaping each individual book in the Writings shared common assumptions about the nature and authority of Torah and Prophets. Rather, a holistic view of the Writings testifies only to an ongoing and diverse dialogue between text and community. It is, finally, that dialogue that becomes normative for all subsequent biblical communities.

Theological Principles

Despite the differences in method that characterize proponents of a canonical approach to biblical literature, there are some significant points of agreement about the overall theological character of the Bible. Most affirm and emphasize diversity. Some, however, discuss this diversity through attention to the different theological structures within the text itself by using intertextuality and other literary methods to illustrate their points and to engage in the hermeneutical task of relating differing theological messages to one another. Others stress the pluralism of the biblical message by focusing attention on the character of community as reflected by the text. Because this pluralism produced, and continues to produce, different theological pictures, methods are used that highlight the changing circumstances and needs of the community as it relates to an authoritative text. The theocentric character of the canon is emphasized by all. For Sanders, the canon represents a consistent concern to "monothesize": to relate new circumstances and revelations to the God of Israel as portrayed, witnessed to, and proclaimed by the stories and stipulations of the Scriptures.[22]

In light of the many methods utilized and the different emphases within their work, a final question concerning the canonical approach is in order. Does the "canonical criticism" of Sanders or the canonical analysis of Childs represent particular and new methodological approaches to the text necessary for the determination of the canonical hermeneutics within the Bible? The answer would appear to be yes and no. To the extent that we focus on either the text or the community, methods are appropriate for the study of each of these entities. By and large, these methods are not new. Rather, form criticism, literary criticism, redaction criticism, comparative midrash, and a host of other "old" approaches are being used to answer "new" questions about the function of authoritative text in the ancient, and contemporary, communities. Although the resultant interpretations of Sanders and Childs are often new and provocative, these results do not demand the use of new methods to achieve them.

What is "new" and central for a study of canonical hermeneutics is its goal, to study the texts and communities in light of canon. For this reason it appears more appropriate to describe the canonical hermeneutics of the Writings as the result of examining text and community *from a different perspective* than with different methods. Such a perspective requires both a holistic reading as well as special attention to the authoritative function of the text within particular communities. When applied to the Writings and subsequent biblical literature, such an approach or perspective provides us with hermeneutical paradigms that continue to be central to all those who use the biblical canon.

TOWARD A CANONICAL HERMENEUTIC
FOR THE WRITINGS

Relying upon the preceding discussion and the work of previous studies, we can outline what a canonical hermeneutic for the Writings will look like in this study. Textual hermeneutics are concerned with both the theory and the modes of interpretation. The present object of such interpretation is the biblical text. The goal is twofold. First, we seek to understand the message of the text through a study of the interpretive principles operative within it. Second, we hope to provide a way of understanding the text that allows the contemporary faith community to participate in a similar interpretive process. The methods of such contemporary interpretation need not be the same as those utilized by biblical authors, but hopefully there is an organic relationship between them. Thus, hermeneutics are both a description of what biblical communities did and a way of understanding the contemporary task as well.

Because a canonical hermeneutic focuses upon both the context of the Writings within the canon and the process that produced it, the authoritative role of this literature as canon will be investigated (chapter 6). In the post-exilic period the concept of canon functions for the Writings primarily as a boundary marker, delineating the texts to be discussed and directing that every historical and literary method available be used to discern the nature of these texts and the communities that produced them. A canonical hermeneutic, as all textual hermeneutics must, presupposes a text and an interpreter as necessary if the interpretive process is to occur. It is more specific, however, because the interpreter is not an individual but a community. Moreover, a canonical hermeneutic presupposes that all communities are responding to and interpreting a common text. Thus, canonical hermeneutics rest upon a common dialogue with a common text.

Despite this common dialogue, the Writings clearly reflect an interpretive process that goes in many different directions. In part, this is the result of the multivalence of the common text. In part, this is the result of the diversity of post-exilic Israel. A canonical hermeneutic of the Writings will therefore consist of many different interpretive paradigms, all witnessing to the dialogue between text and community they share. Ultimately, when canonized, these hermeneutics provide an authoritative text with several different ways to read and live the biblical story for a wide variety of purposes.

To arrive at such a hermeneutic we presuppose a community-text dialogue in post-exilic Israel. Our task is first to determine the nature of the text, Torah-Prophets. Then, recognizing that the particular needs and agendas of the communities in this period provide the motivation for interpreting the text, we will attempt to describe these interpretive communities. Because the text also shapes the community, we must examine the particular ways in which Torah and Prophets are used by post-exilic Israel. The final forms of the literature produced reflect particular interpretive approaches to the text in part controlled and shaped by Torah and Prophets. Tracing the subsequent history of this hermeneutical process for Christian and Jewish canons, discussing the final shape of the Writings as canon, and outlining some of the implications for the task of contemporary theology complete our task. Although much more historical, sociological, literary, and theological study must be done to flesh out the fullness of the hermeneutics presented here, it is hoped we will have at least provided a picture of scripture in community that warrants more study and consideration.

CONCLUSIONS

We have now sketched an understanding of canonical hermeneutics as a basis for studying the post-exilic Writings and later Christian and Jewish literature. Although there has been wide disagreement about canonical methodology and its purpose, we have clarified the guidelines for this study. The Writings are viewed both as a literary canonical division with a special relationship, historically and theologically, to other authoritative scripture, and as the product of many different post-exilic communities with diverse, even divergent, interests. At all times we should focus on the question of how a text was interpreted and functioned authoritatively for a community of faith. The various methods used by Childs, Sanders, and others do not represent many "new" approaches but rather reflect a different perspective, asking questions about canonical function and shape within community rather than asking questions concerning the original author and intention alone. Terminological clarity, especially as it signifies a constructive (canon) or descriptive (scripture) task, is essential. Whether a constructive proposal for contemporary biblical theology is possible using the concept of canon is still to be determined. What is clear, however, are the theological character and concerns of canonical hermeneutics as they attempt to describe the ways in which community and text are in dialogue concerning what God is calling the people to be and do. At no point may the dialogue of text and community, constitutive of canon, be allowed to focus on one or the other exclusively.

A final word is necessary concerning the interrelationship of text and community as presupposed by canon. As an authoritative text, the canon has often been perceived as reflective of the contemporary community's concern to anchor the present in the past. Even the picture of Moses in Deuteronomy can be viewed in this way, with Moses suggesting that to survive in the promised land one must remember, and obey, the old law and story. In fact, however, a canonical dialogue between text and community represents exactly the opposite phenomenon: a received and authoritative text being applied to new situations that demand new interpretations, themselves authoritative, for the community. It is surely true for both Christians and Jews that often the resultant literary structures of canon suggest that only by looking at, for example, the law of Moses may we understand the "new" of Ezra, Jesus, or Paul. However, such a structural picture is dependent upon the "new" as well as the "old." Further, it is the "new" that prompts the dialogue at all. We cannot affirm an enduring and forever valid canonical theology found in the text without a community that brings its world to that text. In that interrelationship and dialogue, both text and community are reshaped in light of the different value systems and the different revelations each brings.

Throughout this chapter we have directed our attention first to the community side of the canonical dialogue. We have done this not because the values and problems that beset the faith community are necessarily the factors that will assume priority in understanding the text, but rather because those problems motivate the task and set it in motion. This study itself is an example of such a canonical dialogue. It would be naive and shortsighted not to recognize the pluralistic nature of our world and the lack of consensus about a "center" for biblical theology as primary motivations for our examination of the Writings in all their diversity.

3

Community Shapes
the Text

The purpose of this chapter is to examine the third division of the Hebrew canon, the Writings, from a holistic perspective. I am concerned with the question of how this literature in all of its diversity may be seen as arising from, and reflecting, a dialogue between authoritative scripture and many different post-exilic communities. I focus upon the nature and character of these post-exilic communities as reflected in the literature they produced. In order to provide a complete picture of the text-community dialogue, one needs to be aware of the agendas and needs of these communities and the literary ways they used to express them. These essential ingredients are necessary for the community to shape the text.

SCRIPTURE AND THE WRITINGS IN
THE POST-EXILIC PERIOD

First, we will delineate the shape and nature of authoritative scripture in the post-exilic period. A brief discussion of the history of the period is necessary in order to understand why early Judaism developed authoritative scriptures and how these functioned in the communities that used them. However, we must go beyond an examination of the historical settings that helped to shape Torah and Prophets and that define in part their functions by focusing on the texts themselves. The authoritative literature of the post-exilic period, as today, was not monolithic or univalent. In order to understand the ways in which Torah and Prophets evoked response, one needs to be aware of the ambivalent, or perhaps multivalent, messages conveyed in the literature, especially when Torah, as a whole, and Prophets, as a whole, are juxtaposed with each other.

A second, and larger, task is to examine the Writings and their communities in the context of this post-exilic period and its authoritative literature. The types of communities and their special interests and goals are integrally related to the types of literature they produce. Again, all of this is to be seen in the light of the authoritative scripture so much a part of their life. Such a task can be achieved only with broad brush strokes. Because our goal is to provide an overview of the character of all the literature in the Writings and to demonstrate a relationship between it and scripture, such a sweeping procedure, with all of its shortcomings, is necessary. In order to accomplish these tasks, we will focus on both community and text, as warranted by our understanding of canonical hermeneutics presented above.

Finally, we conclude with an overview. Certain patterns of biblical interpretation have begun to take form, as reflected in the Writings and the agendas of the communities represented. Although the future shape of the canons of both Christianity and Judaism will be dependent upon subsequent events and developments, they are also to be seen in continuity with the text-community dialogue exemplified in the Writings. For this reason a clear summary will be provided.

This chapter is related to chapter 4, where more attention is given to the ways in which the authoritative texts of Torah and Prophets are actually used by the Writings. The result is the delineation of a number of literary methods and paradigms used by post-exilic Israel as it responds to its scripture. Together, these two chapters should yield a fruitful way to view this literature so that we can understand something of its purpose and function within post-exilic Israel and their importance in helping to define the nature of biblical communities today.

SCRIPTURE

To discuss the history of the post-exilic period of ancient Israel is a difficult task. Our primary literary sources are meager. Moreover, few of these sources have as their main intention a presentation of the historical developments in this period. Even when this is the case, as in the books of Ezra and Nehemiah, the story has been told with very special interests in mind. Events that might give us a more balanced picture are often neglected or distorted. Nevertheless, the biblical literature itself, with all of its biases and lacunae, remains the primary source for our reconstruction of the post-exilic history.

The overview that follows is not intended to be a history of this period. Rather, I want to highlight some of the most important characteristics of these times and to identify the challenges that confronted Israel. All of this forms a backdrop for a discussion of the nature and shape of the authoritative literature that arose. It is critical to recognize that the historical events and community challenges presented are powerful shaping agents not only for Torah and Prophets but for the Writings as well. The implications of this shared history for the foundational texts of Judaism and for the Writings must therefore be discussed at the end of this section.

Historical Overview

The terminology most often used to refer to the period, post-*exilic*, points to a major component of its definition, the exile and its effect upon the subsequent history of Israel. The destruction of the Judean state and especially Jerusalem establishes the framework and many of the central characteristics for understanding this period. The concept of "loss" is central to the exile. Lost was a Judean state with political autonomy. Lost was a monarchy. Lost was a temple and a well-organized and established cult. Lost was any meaningful concept of a centralized worship place.

It is difficult to overestimate the importance of these losses, for the identity of Israel had long been associated with the physical symbols of a king, a cult, and a state, as they reflected notions of God's election and special relationship with this people. The history of the post-exilic period may be seen in part as a series of attempts by Israel to deal with the loss of these physical symbols. Sometimes this was accomplished through rebuilding and restoration. At other times, new conceptions of identity and mission emerged.

The loss of political autonomy signaled another reality of the post-exilic period. Israel was now directly under the control of other nations. Although we must always recognize the organic interrelationship between the people of Palestine and other, often larger, political entities that surround it, the history of Israel during this period is better viewed as a smaller part of Babylonian, Persian, Hellenistic (Egyptian and Syrian), and Roman history; that is, with the exception of the short period following the Maccabean revolt, "Israel" was a part of the empires that surrounded it. Such subjugation had great consequences, both positive and negative, for the people.

Because of Babylonian policies, many Judean citizens were "exiled" to Babylon; others went to Egypt. This phenomenon has left an indelible mark on Judaism (and Christianity) to the present day. Never again would all of "Israel" be found within the physical boundaries of Judah or Palestine. Central to the definition of Judaism would be, and continues to be, its Diaspora character. Some of those who were "dispersed" would never return. The result was that, in the post-exilic period, the Jewish people would consist of communities both inside and outside Palestine. Questions about the centrality of Jerusalem and the relationship of diverse communities in very different cultural settings would forever be a part of defining who, what, and where "Israel" was.

A predictable consequence of the Diaspora was a growing diversity within the people of Israel. Even if common purposes, common authoritative texts, and common assumptions about values could be proposed and adopted by all Jewish communities, it was virtually impossible to live out these purposes, texts, and values in the same way in Babylon, Egypt, and Judah. Moreover, the multivalency of Torah and other authoritative past traditions made it difficult to establish consensus on these types of issues even in a single community. Diversity—of culture, of life-style, of interpretation—would characterize the post-exilic period and all of Judaism's subsequent history.

To these fundamental characteristics of the post-exilic period must be added two others: the waning of prophecy and the establishment of a commonwealth by Ezra and Nehemiah. These developments not only are tied to the emergence of Torah as central to post-exilic Judaism, but also reflect important historical characteristics of the period. The so-called demise of prophecy is in part a response to post-exilic conditions that increasingly signaled to them that God would not act in the history of the people in the same way as in the past. The subjugation of the people to foreign powers and the diversity of voices with no consensus—these created an atmosphere and a worldview with little patience for prophecy in the classical mode. And the reforms of Ezra and Nehemiah, although surely elevating the role and function of Torah in the post-exilic period, also recognized the political realities that had to be built into any definition of "Israel." As such, Ezra and Nehemiah were not simply advocating a new role for scripture but defining the role and shape of Israel in light of present, and apparently (to them), unchangeable social and political realities. These two developments represent a basic characteristic of the post-exilic period, a tension with which all Judaism had to live: the need to accommodate its customs and religious faith to the powers of this world without losing its identity.

These fundamental characteristics of the post-exilic period raised many different questions for the communities of ancient Israel. Who are we? What holds us together? What is our mission? How are we to relate to one another in our diversity? How are we to relate to the nations, to those in power? How can we—or should we—organize ourselves in order to preserve and nurture our identity as the people of God? Of what should our worship consist? What is most important in our stories of the past, and how should it help us in answering questions of identity, survival, and mission? The social and political realities mentioned above both raised these questions and provided a context that could never give rise to answers that would achieve unanimous consent for all of Israel. In other words, the post-exilic period reflects many different questions and many different answers. In view of the Diaspora and a multivalent scriptural tradition, we could hardly expect otherwise.

It is tempting to conclude our discussion of the post-exilic period and its history at this point, with diversity and perhaps even chaos reigning supreme. Yet many students of this period—through a study of biblical and extrabiblical literature as well as physical archaeological evidence—have tried to suggest ways to understand, if not resolve, this diversity. By polarizing the responses made (e.g., theocracy/eschatology; realists/visionaries) or positing a complicated political process among many different "parties," some semblance of order and direction may be "seen." However, such attempts can stretch credulity because the evidence marshaled is often sparse. Moreover, like our present "canonical" approach, they risk reading *later* conceptions of the literature and its intentions back into this period. Thus, as our picture of the post-exilic period has demonstrated, we will turn to the literature of Torah, Prophets, and Writings in order to make sense of the development of Judaism. Such attempts will always be constructions that claim more than the literature gives. My claim is that the present approach is at least congruent and consistent with what little evidence we possess.

Torah and Prophets: Development

To describe the development of scripture in post-exilic Israel is hazardous, although the history of the period we have sketched provides some guidelines. Sanders, for example, views the exile and its aftermath (sixth–fifth centuries) and the destruction of the Second Temple (first century C.E.) as critical periods for canonization. He also sees the

Hellenistic period, especially the second century B.C.E. when proscription of Jewish religious customs occurred, as important.[1] Whether
or not the canon in its present shape actually reflects these periods
and the needs of these particular times is much debated. However,
the crises that confronted Judaism in these periods surely provided
an impetus for the people to define themselves in terms of a central
story, a textual tradition that could be common property shared by
diverse communities throughout the Diaspora. Further, it is difficult
to believe that "Torah" or "Prophets" or "other" authoritative writing
was viewed by all communities as homogeneous or monolithic in either
its content or its structure until quite late in the post-exilic period
and, very possibly, even later.

To explain the development of Torah and Prophets only in terms
of the historical crises of the post-exilic period is not enough. We also
need to recognize that even in the pre-exilic period developments
pushed toward a textual tradition as a central part of the definition of
Israel. The most obvious and perhaps the most important example was
the Deuteronomic movement with its concern to place the "law of
Moses" at the very center of the cult and the monarchial state. Although
centralization of the cult at Jerusalem was motivated by pre-exilic
concerns no longer applicable to all of the new social realities of the
exilic and post-exilic periods, the reliance on a "book" that gave direction and definition for the people continued to be important in
later times. The Deuteronomistic History (Deuteronomy–2 Kings)
represented a way of relating the past, present, and future to the stories
and stipulations found in the central text. Although many different
types of literature would be produced or collected in the post-exilic
period, all of them would need to be related to foundational texts. In
this sense, the development of Torah and Prophets and Writings is to
be seen not simply as responses to "new" events but as a continuation
of older patterns and concerns that focused on the text as central,
rather than on a monarchy, a state, or even a cult.

We have no records of councils, conventions, or synods debating
the scope and content of scripture in the post-exilic period. Nevertheless, the tripartite division of the present canon is usually judged
to reflect accurately the sequential and chronological development of
scripture. Almost all agree that Torah was the central scriptural collection for post-exilic Judaism. Leaving aside the debates over the time
of its exact and final composition, the evidence found in Ezra, Nehemiah, Chronicles, the Psalms, and elsewhere confirms the authoritative place and role of Torah from at least the fourth century B.C.E.

on. In view of the many different communities and cultures represented by Judaism in this period, it would seem likely that Torah itself was not necessarily a "fixed" text identical for all. At the same time, the basic structure (Genesis–Deuteronomy), the elevation of Moses as scribe and prophet and lawgiver par excellence—these would have been common to all Torah communities.

The classical and traditional view of the development of the Prophets maintains that this literature functioned as a collection by the end of the third century B.C.E. The Writings, at least some of them (e.g., the Psalms), are already associated with the Torah and Prophets by the second century B.C.E. as evidenced in the following famous quotation from the Prologue to Ecclesiasticus: "Whereas many great teachings have been given to us through the law and the prophets *and the others that followed them...*" (emphasis added).

Many challenges to this picture have been made by recent scholarship. In addition to the debate over the date when this literature functioned as scripture, there is disagreement about its form. Unlike Torah, whose scope and contents were fairly stable, the literature of the Prophets and Writings appears, to some scholars at least, much more fluid.[2] Although we can recognize that all of the non-Torah scripture of early Judaism was capable of being used prophetically (the Psalms are a classic example), nevertheless, the textual evidence appears to confirm that the "Prophets" represented a scriptural collection to be distinguished as a body from what later was referred to as the Writings. The value of contemporary scholarship that challenges the use of a tripartite division of scripture to describe the post-exilic period lies in its recognition of the simultaneous development of this literature rather than in its conclusion that Jewish communities made no distinction between Prophets and "the others that followed them."

By the end of the second century B.C.E., all of the literature that would become the Hebrew Bible had been composed. Torah and Prophets were stable collections. Some would claim the same for the Writings and maintain the canon was closed.[3] However, with others I would argue for a significantly later date for an official closing of the canon.[4] I do so not on the basis of the scant evidence from official decisions, but rather by an examination of the hermeneutical functions of the Writings and their import for other Jewish and Christian literature. An open-ended canon seems one possible and appropriate way to explain subsequent developments.

Tension between Torah and Prophets

Although our presentation of the development of scripture in the post-exilic period has used the canonical divisions of Torah, Prophets, and Writings to identify and delineate the growth of a body of authoritative literature, we are not describing a history of canonization. That is, although the basic outline of what will become a tripartite canon has its roots in this period, no official decisions were made about "canon" at this time. The following statement by James Kugel reflects a conservative assessment of the status of scripture in this period.

> In the closing centuries before the common era, there probably was no "canon" in the sense in which we use the term. . . . But there surely was a (loosely defined) group of *basic texts,* whose centrality and sacredness were recognized by all, texts like the Pentateuch, which were studied with care and whose words were accepted as decisive for all of Israel. One might say that, if there was not yet a canon in our sense, there probably was at least a *curriculum,* or different curricula, studied by various groups. The gradual process of assembly and manifold decisions that stand behind such curricula—these constitute the major work of canonization; the little acts of inclusion and exclusion that come later are of a far lesser order.[5]

To this statement, we would add the observation that the centrality of Torah and Prophets was an important theological and organizational reality with which all early Judaism had to deal. It is the way in which post-exilic Judaism perceived and responded to Torah and Prophets, as reflected in the Writings, that is responsible for the present tripartite canon and the hermeneutics bequeathed to subsequent Jewish and Christian communities.

It has often been noted that the development of a central and authoritative literary corpus raises serious problems of interpretation in light of the many different needs represented by post-exilic Judaism in its several settings. It is not only different historical situations that create the necessity of different approaches to scripture but also the texts themselves. Torah and Prophets are multivalent. They represent the collected agendas of many earlier communities struggling with mission, definition of community, and how to remain faithful to the God of Israel. Although contemporary biblical scholarship can usually identify a final structure and perspective that is intended to govern our interpretation of a particular book or perhaps even a canonical division such as Torah, traces of other and earlier perspectives are not erased. Moreover, it appears naive to assume that post-exilic Judaism would attempt to read Torah from the perspective of the Priestly code only, or the "Former Prophets" (Joshua–2 Kings) only through the eyes of the Deuteronomist. Rather, the many different methods and results of scriptural interpretation in this period are a testimony both to the needs of widely divergent communities and to the multivalence of the scriptures they held in common.

In addition to the problems of determining the meaning and pertinence of Torah or Prophets, there is fundamental tension between these two different scriptural collections. Torah, with its focus on a basic story and identity of Israel, and its emphasis on following the revealed will of God as found in the law of Moses, can be seen as the "constitution" of post-exilic Judaism. We must agree with Sanders and others who point to the adaptability, even the flexibility, of Torah.[6] At the same time, Torah witnesses to stability, to a community ideal that emphasizes the "here and now." As such, Torah values the status quo wherever possible and has often been used by community builders who seek to create and legitimate existing social structures.

The Prophets, although dependent upon the basic story and values of Torah, witness to another experience of Israel—the inbreaking of the new and the unexpected, the continuing revelation of a God who will not always be bound by the past, even by Torah. Although in Torah Moses becomes the prophet par excellence, and as such for all of scripture, the radical changes called for by the prophets who follow him cannot always be embraced by the structures of a Torah-obedient community. Future visions of a messiah and a people of God with different social and cultic structures may create tension when juxtaposed with community visions based upon Torah alone.

To characterize Torah and Prophets in this way is in part simplistic and unfair to the texts themselves, for Torah contains many future-oriented messages, and the Prophets contain many status quo visions. Nevertheless, the tension between a present that must care about community organization in its day-to-day living and a future that brings the unexpected, even a potential transformation or destruction of present social structures, is epitomized by a comparison of these two collections of authoritative literature. When the difficult and dangerous situations of the post-exilic period are added to this inherent tension within scripture itself, the scene is set for a diversity of interpretation and for a multifold response to the questions, Who are we? and What is God calling us to be and do? Some will focus on the present, attempting to build community on the basis of the fundamental stories and stipulations as found in Torah. Others, while taking that story seriously, as all Israel must, will continue to dream dreams, to speak of a God who can, will, and must deliver the people—even if such a deliverance results in the destruction or a radical transformation of existent community structures based upon Torah.

Into such a historical and literary context—filled with different expectations, hopes, and needs, and a literary context, marked by a multivalent scripture in tension with itself—the Writings must be placed. This literature, viewed as a whole, reflects a series of inter-relationships with Torah, Prophets, and the complicated and difficult settings of the post-exilic period.

THE WRITINGS

The growth of a central textual tradition composed of Torah and Prophets in the midst of a period characterized by a lack of consensus on issues of identity and mission for Israel—this created an atmosphere virtually guaranteed to produce diverse responses. Needs for both stability and adaptability in light of multivalent texts and a multicultural Judaism are reflected in the Writings.

To understand the function of the Writings, viewed individually and as a whole, we need to recognize the many different ways it is possible to respond to Torah and Prophets as well as the diverse situations and needs represented by the communities that composed them. The community (post-exilic)–text (Torah and Prophets) dialogue presupposed by a discussion of canonical hermeneutics is the foundation for explicating the role of this literature. When the Writings are viewed holistically, the responses made can be arranged into categories that represent particular needs of the community and particular literary formulations consonant with those needs. No one community, no one literary response found in the Writings wins the day and becomes the only way to "be" Israel. However, when *all* responses are viewed together, grouped according to their similar agendas and their liter-ature, a morphology of a biblical community is created. That biblical community, shaped by its diverse interpretations of a common textual tradition, provides a major hermeneutical paradigm for both Judaism and Christianity in the future.

Before a presentation of the responses found in the Writings is given, two observations and qualifications are necessary. First, the ways in which Torah and Prophets, the central textual tradition of post-exilic Israel, are manifested in the Writings are as diverse as the literature itself. Sometimes Torah and Prophets permeate the literature that responds to them and are found in every crevice and crack. The Psalms, Ezra–Nehemiah, and 1–2 Chronicles are good examples, for without Torah and Prophets it is difficult if not impossible to conceive of this later literature at all. In other cases, such as wisdom literature, we will not find explicit and frequent references to Torah and Prophets. Yet, by examining the roles of the writers and the needs of their particular communities, it can be argued that even here we may find an important testimony to the central role of scripture in the growth of a scribal class so necessary for its interpretation and transmission. Direct citation or reference to a central text is not the only or even the primary way in which a text-centered community lives out its mission. The histories of Judaism and Christianity are replete with illustrations of such a phenomenon, as found, for example, in the Talmudic teachings of the sages.

Second, although we believe the function and message of the Writings are illuminated by the presupposition of a shared response to Torah and Prophets in this period, we also recognize that no conceptual system adequately explains all of the textual and historical evidence; that is, no "system" or hermeneutical paradigm is adequate to the task, for always something does not quite fit, and defies all our attempts to synthesize and explain. Such a recognition, of course, is congruent with both the history and the literature itself. The diversity of the Writings, however successfully we may organize it, still witnesses to the lack of consensus, the inability to agree upon what should be central to Judaism, in this period. This lack of consensus, always in dialogue with a basic and common story, ultimately becomes the theological and hermeneutical gift of the Writings to the biblical communities that follow.[7]

Sages and Wisdom

The wisdom literature in the Writings includes Proverbs, Ecclesiastes, and Job. Although the most fundamental literary form of these writers is the *mashal*, or proverb, several other forms are used. Dialogue (Job), autobiographical reminiscence (Ecclesiastes), longer poems about wisdom and virtue (Proverbs and Job), allegory (Ecclesiastes), admonitions, and numerical sayings are all common to this aphoristic literature.

Although sapiential sayings are found throughout the Hebrew Bible and witness to the importance of this way of thinking and speaking in all times and places in Israel, this literature has often posed difficulties for the biblical theologian.[8] Despite its use of creation and a retributional theological system compatible with, for example, Deuteronomy, the relationship between wisdom literature and the more foundational theological perspectives found in Torah and Prophets has often defied adequate description by commentators. This literature focuses its attention on everyday experience rather than on more dramatic forms of revelation (e.g., Sinai or oracles) and rarely provides a rationale for the moral life grounded in the stories and history of God's action in the life of Moses, David, or others. The fact that the authors of this literature are, by and large, anonymous and difficult to locate within a social matrix further contributes to the problem.[9]

This literature primarily answers the question of how to live life to its fullest and its best. Although Job and Ecclesiastes, in quite different ways, reflect a lack of consensus on the part of the wisdom tradition about how such life and the God who gives it are to be viewed, nevertheless, the teachers and writers of wisdom are all engaged in a search for and an explanation of the fundamental order of life as given by God. More often than not, wisdom writing maintains a conservative, even a status quo, approach to the created order as manifested in and legitimated by contemporary social structures.

In pre-exilic times, the locus of wisdom literature has usually been associated with either the family or the monarchy. Although Ecclesiastes and Proverbs have nominal connections with the monarchy, post-exilic circumstances press us to search for another provenance in this later period. To be sure, the family may have provided an impetus for the continuation of wisdom teaching and writing. The growing importance of a central and authoritative literary tradition appears, however, to offer an even more significant and satisfying explanation for this literature. The communities of post-exilic Israel were faced with "new" challenges and needs that wisdom teachers were uniquely qualified to meet. Texts needed to be written and preserved, to be edited, corrected, or adapted. Given the importance of the Deuteronomic movement and its theological compatibility with the "two ways" system of wisdom, those literati with skills and ability both to write and preserve and to teach and interpret became very important.[10] Moreover, the old concern to educate provided an essential connection between the sages and the authors of Torah and Prophets.

Yet, in spite of the compatibility between sages and the scripture of post-exilic Israel, we are still unable to provide a clear social matrix for these teachers. The fact that their way of speaking, and their roles as interpreters of the written word permeate other literature in the

Writings such as Esther and Daniel surely witnesses to their presence. Until the time of Ben Sira, however, evidence for "schools" or other loci for the training and teaching of scribes and sages is sparse. By the end of the post-exilic period, that the scribe and sage had become a central authority in Judaism appears clear. Perhaps the role of Ezra as "scribe" reflects the locus for these teachers-interpreters-preservers. Surely we must explain at least some of the redactional activity found in Torah and Prophets to scribes.[11] By the time of Ben Sira and the Wisdom of Solomon, "wisdom" is firmly associated with Torah. This development, coupled with the functional importance of scribes and sages as interpreters, writers, and teachers, is an essential antecedent for the future place of sages and rabbis in Judaism.

In summary, the wisdom literature in the Writings represents a major response to Torah and Prophets in the post-exilic period. The growth and development of a central textual tradition brought with it the need to transmit, preserve, teach, and interpret. For these writers, the focus was on living, on making sense of their experience in the light of a God-given order. Passing on the teachings of earlier writers and teachers, the wisdom authors of the Writings did not themselves make the giant step of equating their experientially based wisdom with Torah—although the epilogue to Ecclesiastes and the final verses of Hosea point in this direction. Nevertheless, the questions posed by wisdom and the answers given are compatible with those who used Torah and Prophets more directly and explicitly in the post-exilic period. By the end of this period, these often anonymous writers had become a crucial part of the Jewish community, essential for the maintenance and continuance of Torah, Prophets, and Writings.

Singers and Psalms

The wisdom literature of the Writings reflects the concerns of a relatively small class of scribes and sages essential for the future interpretation and transmission of scripture. Psalms and Lamentations, in contrast, represent settings and concerns common to all community members in the post-exilic period. This poetry, in a variety of forms, reflects the need for worship and the many different ways and places in which such worship can occur. Lament, praise, confession, and meditation are used by the community to speak of and to continue its relationship with God. This literature calls Israel to remember, to question, and to pray in the context of worship. Like wisdom literature, psalms are found in all parts of the Hebrew Bible. Unlike wisdom literature, psalms are easily identified with an activity central and basic to Israel at all times: the worship life of the community wherever it finds itself. Psalms integrate past, present, and future. They speak of and are often attributed to great figures in Israel's story (David, Miriam, Moses, Deborah). They mandate that the present community of faith be engaged in the same activities of praise and lament by using old songs and by composing new ones. Such an activity provides a means by which the worshiping community may remain faithful to the God who has brought them to the present and who leads them into the future.

Of all the literature in the Writings, the Psalms most clearly function as scripture, as authoritative texts, alongside Torah and Prophets in the post-exilic period. Indeed, many of these songs and prayers have their origin long before the exile and its aftermath. The Psalms in their present form, however, represent particular needs and a specific response to the events of this later period. Although a need for cultic organization is common to all periods in ancient Israel, it is especially important when the cult becomes the primary institution and the state is no longer extant. For example, Psalm titles witness to a variety of groups charged with the responsibility of composing prayers and organizing worship for many different occasions. Such activity and responsibilities were a common concern to Jews wherever they found themselves. This literature suggests that liturgy and worship were at the center of all post-exilic communities. They represent a need common to all—to praise and, perhaps more often, to lament.

Unlike wisdom literature, the psalmody of post-exilic Israel is filled with references to Torah and Prophets. Without this central authoritative literature, there could be no worship, no Israel. Sometimes the community is called to remember the acts of God and to praise; sometimes to remember and lament. In all cases the people are to maintain their relationship with the God of Moses, David, the prophets. To achieve this goal, the psalmists often adapted songs of old for their new and radically different circumstances. Thus, enthronement psalms of the past became messianic in character, or psalms of trust became psalms of hope and expectation.

In addition to the adaptation of old psalms to new circumstances, post-exilic Israel composed new prayers and meditations reflecting the centrality of Torah in the community. Torah psalms (1, 119) and wisdom psalms (37, 49) are examples of later psalmody attempting to relate all of Israel's worship to its authoritative scripture. The heavy preponderance of lament psalms also reflects the post-exilic response to Torah and Prophets. This period had much justification for lamentation and confession; and a retributional theology explaining why and how God acts on behalf of or against the people needed to be related to similar perspectives found in Torah and the Prophets.

The Psalms and Lamentations represent a significant response to emergent scripture in the post-exilic period. They were collected and organized by a special group within each community charged with this responsibility. All of the agendas and interest groups of post-exilic Israel are found in the Psalms. The knowledge and use of past traditions suggest that the cult proclaims and preserves the Torah and Prophets, with the help of specially trained scribes and sages. Indeed, some of the later psalms appear to have been written by those with sapiential perspectives. Finally, however, this literature witnesses to a central context in which the dialogue between text and community will, and must, occur: the worshiping community. Above all, the Psalms are prayers and meditations addressed to God in the midst of worship. If Torah and Prophets and the people of Israel are to survive, a necessary instrument for that survival is to be found in worship. That worship, as reflected in the Psalms, is as socially and theologically diverse as post-exilic Israel. Nevertheless, the centering function, the call to worship, the integration of past, present, and future—all of this witnesses to a common activity for all of early Judaism.

Community Builders and Torah-History

A third response to the challenges faced by post-exilic Judaism is found in the books of 1–2 Chronicles, Ezra, and Nehemiah. Viewed as a whole, these texts present the history of Israel from its very beginnings to the time of Ezra and Nehemiah. The history of the monarchial period, significant omissions from and additions to earlier sources, is recounted in 1–2 Chronicles. It is usually seen as an important midrash or commentary reflecting the special needs and concerns of later times. Ezra and Nehemiah, however, present a picture of the early post-exilic period with special interests in the roles of its leaders for the formation of community.

The monarchial period of Judah is the special focus of 1–2 Chronicles; the post-exilic period and the activities of Ezra and Nehemiah are the primary concern of the books that bear their names. The sources for this history are many and varied. Letters, lists, genealogies, and the Deuteronomistic History (especially 1–2 Samuel and 1–2 Kings) are adapted for the primary purpose of building community.

Until rather recently, the consensus view of biblical scholarship regarded this literature as the product of one school of thought or even one hand, commonly referred to as the "Chronicler." Renewed study of the language, sources, and theological perspectives of Ezra–Nehemiah and 1–2 Chronicles, however, has suggested an alternative thesis of two sources or authors responsible for these literary complexes. Given the different emphases upon David and the prophets (1–2 Chronicles), and Moses and Torah (Ezra–Nehemiah), we believe that such a distinction is appropriate whether or not it is the result of different "sources" or merely representative of one community's different appropriation of Torah and Prophets. Such different emphases may be seen as a natural result of the tension between Torah and Prophets.

If the Psalms and Lamentations witness to the need for integration of emergent scripture into a worship context, the literature of Ezra–Nehemiah and 1–2 Chronicles witnesses to the interrelationship of scripture with the political processes that control and govern the life of the community of faith. Such processes control more than internal matters of leadership and the organization of the Temple cult. They also involve the community's relationship with the Persian state and with the foreigners or non-Jews who live in or near the environs of Jerusalem. All aspects of the province in which Palestinian Jews were found—from religious life to public works—were affected by political factors.

After more than a century of foreign domination and a variety of proposals for community identity and organizations that failed to bring consensus, the time was ripe for community builders such as Ezra and Nehemiah. Indeed, without three aspects—strong leadership, a place for community organization and resultant identity, and the ability to provide a means of differentiating "Israel" from and, at the same time, relating it to its neighbors—the future of the people was in jeopardy.[12] Although the solution seemed—and seems—for some to be too particularistic, too "orthodox," or too intolerant of foreign influence within the community organization, we must look to Ezra and Nehemiah and the authors of the literature of the community builders if the continued existence and a blueprint capable of providing a future for the people are to be explained. Essential to the solution of the community builders was Jerusalem and its cult as the center for all Jews, wherever they lived. Central also was a concern for purity, differentiation, and an organization that affirmed and even mandated that such concerns define the identity of the people of God.

The special genius of these community builders and the literature they produced lay not in their political acumen and organizational insight alone, however, but rather in their ability to ground such insight and acumen in the sacred traditions of the past as found in Torah and Prophets. Ezra becomes a Moses figure, a lawgiver, and a skilled interpreter of the Torah, regardless of the debates over whether or not his "law" was actually Torah in its final form. Similarly David, with all his connections to Moses and the prophets, becomes the architect of the Temple cult. In this literature both Torah and Prophets were made integral to the community and provided the necessary authority and paradigms for its present and future organization and mission.

The means of presentation in these texts reflect the dialogue between text and community. With its primary source being the Deuteronomistic History, the author of 1–2 Chronicles rewrites that history by focusing on the needs of the post-exilic community but retaining the important authority of its source for the organization and identity proposed. Similarly Ezra–Nehemiah, while presenting the central roles of these two community leaders, is concerned to legitimate their actions by making them congruent with and dependent upon Moses and Torah. The result was a Torah-centered community capable of differentiating from and relating itself to those who were not a part of Israel. In such a community sages and others able to interpret Torah and Prophets have a crucial role. In such a community those singers and cultic officials charged with responsibilities for worship are also essential. In this sense, then, the literature of the community builders is inclusive of the authors and concerns found in wisdom literature and the Psalms.

The solution of the community builders, however necessary and important it would become for future Judaism, was still only one answer to the problems faced in the post-exilic period. Questions of organization, differentiation, and an ability to relate to foreign powers had to be addressed if Judaism was to survive. However, the tension between a community concerned to create a stable social structure and identity, on the one hand, and a collection of sacred texts that constantly challenged every interpretation and status quo, on the other hand, continued. Thus, the paradigm of Ezra as interpreter contained within it the seeds of future, and different, interpretations of community. The paradigm of David as architect of the cult contained within it the hope, perhaps even the promise, that God could and would come again, with new visions and new challenges for the people. As such, the programs of the community builders would always remain an unfinished agenda.

Visionaries and Apocalyptic

Within the Writings, the book that reflects most clearly the literature and perspective of the visionaries is Daniel. This type of literature has antecedents in the Prophets (i.e., Isaiah 24–27, 56–66; Zechariah 9–12; Joel) and will become a major way of responding to and interpreting scripture in the period from 200 B.C.E.. to 200 C.E. in extrabiblical writing.

Most of the visionary literature, including Daniel, is associated with the term "apocalypse." Although this term ("vision" or "disclosure," usually associated with "end" times) is sometimes used to characterize one whole form of literature, many quite different literary components may be discerned in an apocalypse or in apocalyptic literature. Thus, for example, the Book of Daniel contains not simply dream narratives, but prayers (2, 9), midrashic commentary (9), and court tales (1–6).

Apocalyptic literature—Daniel in particular—is characterized by dualism (the "good" versus the "evil") that points to important theological (God versus Satan) and social (intracommunity divisions as well as "Israel" versus the "nations" or world) distinctions. Angelology, pseudonymity, and numerology are also important characteristics of this book. The visionary character of the work provides a heavily future-oriented and eschatological flavor to the book. However, such a perspective should not prevent us from seeing the strong implications this type of literature has for present community behavior.

The Book of Daniel is grouped together with the Prophets in the Septuagint, perhaps in part because of the apocalyptic types of literature those books contain. Both the differing placements of this book within canonical collections and the fact that chapters 2–7 are written in Aramaic reflect a long and complex history of composition and transmission within different post-exilic communities. The difficulty in interpreting and placing Daniel in this early period continues to be reflected today both in the canonical placement of the book and in scholarship that debates the relationship of Daniel to the prophets and wisdom.

Much has been written about the type of community that produces apocalyptic literature.[13] The Book of Daniel, although its literary setting is in the Diaspora, is usually associated with events in and around Jerusalem, probably in the Hellenistic period of the mid-second century B.C.E. Such a time was characterized by persecution, proscription of religious practices, programs of accommodation advocated by some Jewish religious leaders, and resultant internal strife within Palestinian Judaism. Despite the accomplishments of Ezra and Nehemiah, Judaism was undergoing severe challenges to its identity as a worshiping community centered in obedience to Torah. For some within the community, new explanations for Hellenistic oppression and guidance for responses to it were needed. Such explanations and responses would provide solace and new direction while at the same time create divisions, and the formation of new communities, within Judaism itself.

Daniel reflects two basic needs on the part of these visionaries. Chapters 1–6 present a picture of Daniel and others as faithful worshipers, obedient even unto death. Such a picture represents a paradigm of behavior that must be lived out. Rather than accommodate and adjust, this visionary community must remain faithful to the past. However, obedience to Torah in the face of persecution had to be accompanied by some explanation, some justification, of the goal of such behavior. Chapters 7–12, with their visions of the end and their promise that the righteous would, ultimately, prevail through God's dramatic intervention, provide such a rationale for those presently suffering persecution from their oppressors, both Jews and Greeks. Although obedience and faithfulness are to be grounded in a direction provided by Torah and Prophets, the "visions" of Daniel are equally necessary for the community to persevere and to understand the present.

In all probability, the community of visionaries represented by the Book of Daniel was small. Its radical social stance probably alienated it from both Seleucids and the more accommodating Jewish establishment. Its authority was legitimated through the figure of Daniel, a pious believer who had been given special abilities to "see" and to interpret the future actions of God. In light of the growth in importance of the scribe or sage in a progressively "book"- or scripture-oriented community, it is hardly surprising that Daniel should be an interpreter par excellence, grounded in the piety of Torah obedience and, at the same time, should provide authoritative visions of the future as did the prophets before him.

The visionary literature of Daniel within the Writings reflects one more way in which post-exilic Israel responded to both the crises of their times and the Torah-Prophets scripture so much a part of the community definition. Seeking to remain faithful to Torah and its demand for obedience and allegiance, Daniel provided strong warrant for a scripturally based civil disobedience while at the same time suggesting that such action might, as with Daniel himself, result in prosperity and power. The precedent of another seer-government administrator, Joseph, is surely a parallel from Torah that might have come to mind. At the same time, the call to obedience found in Daniel is ultimately tied to a new and dramatic inbreaking of God's action that would both fulfill the words of earlier prophets like Jeremiah and turn the world upside down. Nothing less than such visions could explain the disparity between present affliction and the promises of land and the good life found in Torah-Prophets.

The figure of Daniel should not be equated with Moses, with the prophets of old, or with the sages. Rather, he is a composite of all three: a faithful follower of the law, a receiver of revelations to be given to the people, and one given special gifts of discernment and knowledge that enable him to explicate their message to the few who, by their actions and particular allegiance to God, are to be recipients of this special message. On the one hand, Daniel, through his name and actions, stands with Joseph and the prophets. On the other hand, Daniel as a sage represents the authoritative post-exilic scribal tradition through which the meaning of Torah and the Prophets is given. Thus the visionary Book of Daniel points backward to the basic scriptures, Torah and Prophets, and forward to the ongoing process of interpretation to which these scriptures must be subject if they are to provide direction for the present.

In attempting to locate the community of Daniel and the visionaries who produced it, it is tempting to juxtapose and polarize the views of this literature against those found within the more orthodox and accommodating communities represented by the literature of Ezra and Nehemiah.[14] Despite a more radical social stance, even resulting in intracommunal strife, a polarization between visionaries and the "majority" appears unwarranted and simplistic. At least in terms of Torah and Prophets, many common if not always compatible attitudes toward scriptural centrality and its interpretation may be found.

Storytellers and Diaspora Living

In addition to literature that can readily be associated with particular social groups, with specific agendas, and with Torah and Prophets, the Writings also contain two stories, Ruth and Esther, that reflect a less obvious but equally important phenomenon in the scriptural communities of post-exilic Israel: Both narrate their respective heroine's ability to overcome adversity and to achieve ultimate success. Also like the Book of Daniel, each of these stories includes other, non-narrative types of material. Ruth concludes with two genealogies firmly connecting her to the ancestral line of David; Esther contains a festal legend explaining the feast of Purim. Thus these two stories witness to the importance of storytelling, to the paradigmatic value of the actions and lives of their heroines for faithful living, as well as to incorporating other, perhaps initially separate, concerns into such stories.[15]

Both Esther and Ruth are narrative prose. Their precise literary genre definitions continue to be debated (novella, short story, folktales, and so forth have been suggested). Although some date the story of Ruth in the pre-exilic period, a consensus of scholarship maintains a post-exilic setting for the composition of both books. The Moabite lineage of Ruth creates some tension when juxtaposed to certain Torah traditions, and the "secular" flavor of Esther has often been used to denigrate the value of this story. Perhaps partially because of this flavor, Esther in particular has a rich and complex history of transmission, reflected in its septuagintal form and its several different literary components. Although much value is in both books, Esther and Ruth remain for the most part anomalous heroines and subjects for post-exilic storytelling.

If the particular communities that produced and transmitted these stories remain veiled, their intentions and literary provenance do not. The lives and actions of Ruth and Esther must be related to the communities that heard them. These heroines are confronted with particular problems: for Ruth, the loss of family and potential disenfranchisement in a foreign (Israel!) land; and for Esther, political intrigue and the threat of annihilation. What can be generalized is not the ways in which each heroine deals with adversity; their ultimate success and their ability to live good and important lives are morals for all who hear them. When such powerful stories are connected to other authoritative traditions (e.g., David) or to liturgical celebrations of deliverance in a foreign land, their significance for contemporary communities of faith becomes great indeed.

Although we cannot identify the authors of these stories with precision, much suggests a scribe/sage circle as responsible for their transmission in their final forms.[16] In addition to the vocabulary, the court setting (Esther), and other connections, both of these stories are concerned to demonstrate how to live the good life, how to succeed, how to choose wisely, so much a part of the sages' teaching. Although eventually the sages will be associated primarily with the exposition,

interpretation, and transmission of Torah, much in the post-exilic period suggests that their interests and roles in society were broader at
this time. Whether or not we should attribute Ruth and Esther to a
scribally oriented intelligentsia, the concerns of these books appear
to be compatible with such groups.

Despite their common features, there are some glaring differences
between the books of Esther and Ruth. Ruth, on the one hand, presents
an inclusive, even universalistic, picture of Israel. This is in stark contrast with the perspectives found in Ezra–Nehemiah, for example.
Esther, on the other hand, is much more nationalistic in its focus,
although it does not affirm the strict Torah-centered particularism of
Ezra–Nehemiah, as its addition of a non-Torah feast demonstrates. Ruth
can be viewed as a protest against a narrowly defined Judaism, whereas
Esther depends on just such a definition to maintain its nationalism
and the validity of a threat to Jews living in Diaspora. Thus, Ruth and
Esther do not reflect the same community or the same needs. Each
represents a very diverse post-exilic Judaism attempting to respond
to the different challenges of the times in quite different, but legitimate,
ways.

Although Ruth and Esther contain very few explicit references to
Torah and Prophets, they represent important responses to scripture
in this period. Moreover, these stories reflect a dialogue between the
interpretive communities represented by the Writings rather than
direct responses to the primary texts of Torah and Prophets. Hence,
Ruth can be seen as a corrective to a rigid and too particularistic notion
of identity as found, for example, in Ezra–Nehemiah. Esther represents
a call for continuing openness to new rituals and celebrations (Purim)
as responses to new events and situations in post-exilic Israel.

At the same time, Ruth and Esther do emphasize the importance of
traditions within Torah and Prophets. Both stories contain parallels
between the paradigmatic actions of figures such as the trickster Jacob,
the successful "foreign" bureaucrat Joseph, and their respective heroines. The Book of Ruth, which intends to glorify David, has parallels
with Torah, the Deuteronomistic history, and the classical prophets.
Positing two sources for Ezra–Nehemiah and 1–2 Chronicles, Ruth
can be seen affirming the inclusive and Davidic-oriented books of
Chronicles, while warning against the dangers of a rigid interpretation
of Ezra–Nehemiah. Esther, despite no explicit references to Torah, has
an important precedent and parallel with this literature, as it provides
an etiological explanation for contemporary worship practices. The
addition to the festal calendar is at once a bold new stroke by Diaspora

Judaism that ironically rests upon Torah as justifying such a development.

The character of these stories is different from previous responses to Torah and Prophets. Unlike the Psalms, Ezra–Nehemiah, or Daniel, no "answers" are provided. Rather, the behavior of the characters provides paradigmatic actions and situations, which the reader or hearer is to ponder. The success of this behavior may provide an impetus for similar behavior in analogous situations or may simply testify to the value of faithfulness and allegiance to God and Judaism. However they were employed, these stories represent a significant response to the problems and challenges of post-exilic Judaism. Ultimately, they are to be placed alongside other writings that have more explicit references to the central and authoritative scripture, Torah and Prophets.

PARADIGMS FOR THE FUTURE

Viewed from one perspective, the literature of the Writings composed or put into final form in the post-exilic period does not represent a new phenomenon for the people of Israel. The types of literature produced (e.g., aphoristic, liturgical, historical) have antecedents stretching far back into monarchical and even premonarchical times. Moreover, although the new crises that confronted the people were critical in determining their identity, mission, and future, similar claims can be made for the exodus, judges, and monarchical periods. As we have attempted to show, the composite and tension-filled collections of Torah and Prophets are themselves a microcosm of earlier community attempts to discern God's will and to determine appropriate definitions of identity and mission from patriarchal times to the early post-exilic period. Whatever is distinctive about the Writings and the post-exilic period needs to be viewed within a framework that allows for continuity because in many important ways the Writings are not new.

Viewed from another perspective, however, the Writings do represent something new: the beginning of a process responsible for the present shape of Jewish and Christian scriptural canons. More important, perhaps, the process begun by and represented in the Writings reflects a dialogue between community and a fixed, authoritative text that continues to be at the heart of what it means to be a community of the "word." We will argue that the types of literature and the agendas of the post-exilic communities that produced them represent important paradigms for future biblical communities in appropriating their scripture. Nevertheless, the most important legacy of these communities is not the particular ways in which they responded to Torah and Prophets but the fact that they did at all! This is what is really new in the post-exilic period: that a people separated by space, time, and diverse visions of what God was doing with and to Israel used a common scripture as one central part of determining their way of living together and apart. The fact that these literary responses themselves became scripture, in all their continuity with the past and all their diversity with each other and the scripture they held in common, bequeathed to all subsequent Jewish and Christian interpretive communities both a common reference point *and* the right to be different and still be a part of "Israel," the people of God.

However, many of these observations take us beyond the concerns of our present chapter. At the end of the post-exilic period, we are still at the beginning of this "new" development. It is fairly certain that all of the literature in the Writings had not yet attained scriptural status for all of Judaism, and even more certain that it had not been entirely collected into a third section of the canon. However, the dialogue between community and text that would ultimately result in such a phenomenon had begun.

COMMUNITY AND TEXT

The literature of the Writings reflects the agendas of many different communities in Israel and in the Diaspora. When the Writings are viewed as a whole, it seems inappropriate to suggest that the history of this period is a history of solitary and homogeneous communities, each with their clearly defined agendas. Rather, the perspectives and concerns of the psalmists must be related to the sages and the community builders, the storytellers must be related to the sages, and so on. The Writings vividly demonstrate a process of cross-fertilization between Diaspora and non-Diaspora communities and between those who are concerned to build social structures in Jerusalem and those concerned to provide paradigms for faithful living in the Diaspora.

Despite the interrelatedness of agenda and social groupings in the post-exilic period, the Writings also testify to distinctive ways in which these agendas and social groups express themselves. One group, the sages, attempt to deal with the issue of how to live life successfully by focusing on retributional theology and creation. The crises of the times often lead these thinkers into the area of theodicy. A second group that writes psalms and focuses on the liturgical life of the community is concerned to bring the present life of the people into a dynamic dialogue with the past and make that past come alive in worship. Through worship the people are able to center themselves, finding or affirming their identity as God's people through lament and praise. The community builders as a third group—dependent upon both sages for their teaching and their literacy expertise and the psalmists for their call to remember and reactualize the stories of old—are concerned with larger programs. They look ahead to build community around authoritative and centralized structures that will, they hope, provide a focus for identity and mission and will guarantee the continued existence of Israel. Although the visionaries are heirs of the sages, singers, and community builders, something has gone awry. Both new persecution and failure of the whole community to live out the mandates of God have called for the reaffirmation of paradigms for faithful living. Explanations given by this fourth group of how and when God will act on behalf of his chosen people, viewed as a relatively small group, must be provided in visions of the end, intelligible only to the elect. Finally, in part a response to other developments within post-exilic communities, the storytellers as a fifth group affirm the value of paradigms for faithful living while at the same time debating whether nationalism or a more inclusive and universalistic vision of the people is the appropriate vision for Israel in the future. Ultimately both of these options are affirmed, or held in tension by scripture, although it is far from clear at the end of the period in which the Writings are composed whether such a perspective is espoused by all. In summary, community in the Writings is a diverse, even disparate, phenomenon. What appears to hold these groups together is not the many commonalities of their respective agendas or the fact that many, particularly the sages, have similar roles in society, but rather their attempts to relate different concerns and visions to a common textual tradition.

The ways in which the communities of post-exilic Israel express themselves in literature are as diverse as the agendas and social situations they represent. Aphoristic literature of many types—psalms, historical writing, visions, and stories—are all present. Of these, the wisdom literature and the stories of Ruth and Esther are characterized by little direct reference to the scripture of Torah and Prophets. Yet *all* of this literature depends upon Torah-Prophets for its values. At the same time, the new situations of this period often call for new responses, new visions, new stories, new solutions to the problems of the people. The tension and diversity within this literature are at once the product of a common response to a multivalent scripture *and* reflective of the new needs of particular groups with their own special, differing problems and challenges. When viewed as a whole, the texts of the Writings both reflect the diversity of the time and point forward to a scripture that will make such diversity normative.

TOWARD CANON

The Writings contain all the components necessary to explain the shape and nature of a diverse, pluralistic canon, although it would remain the task of others to complete the work begun by these communities. These books arise from and reflect a social situation in which many different responses to questions of identity and mission are not only sanctioned but also are demanded. Ultimately, when grouped together, these books represent a common, if diverse, response to one body of literature. The community-text dialogue represented by Torah-Prophets and Writings will become central for Judaism and Christianity, although the resultant canons will differ.

In light of the evidence, the most important social group in this period would appear to be the sages. This group—with its concern for right living, its theological perspective so in tune with Deuteronomic thinking, its close connection to the central institutions and texts, its growing importance as interpreters and transmitters—comes as close as any to being the common denominator in a social analysis of the Writings. Although the diverseness of literature and agenda prevents any simple and homogeneous description of the sages in post exilic literature, their particular interests and abilities will become increasingly important to all, especially with the emergence of a community of the book.

Speaking of the "winners" and "losers" in post-exilic Judaism has become popular. No doubt this is a legitimate endeavor if we examine the overall goals of these communities retrospectively. In one sense, Ezra and Nehemiah "win." But at the end of the post-exilic period the question of winning or losing is still at issue. There are still many ways to be Israel, still many ways to interpret scripture, still many visions to be experienced, still many "writings" to be written and to be incorporated into authoritative tradition, and still many canonical decisions to be made. Winning and losing are always a matter of perspective, and there were many legitimate perspectives at the end of the post-exilic period, as epitomized in the Writings. It is the heritage of these communities and their literature that, when canon is finally determined and shaped, many perspectives will be included, bequeathing a picture of scriptural communities with a variety of winning and losing viewpoints, held together not by their inherent rightness or wrongness, but by their faithful attempt to relate community to scripture.

4

The Text Shapes Community

The purpose of this chapter is to examine how Torah and Prophets, the basic and authoritative texts of post-exilic Israel, were used in and influenced the literature of the Writings. To accomplish this, three different but related foci will be explored. First, explicit references to Torah and Prophets will be identified. Second, the ways in which this scripture is used and interpreted will be explicated. Third, the resultant shape of the texts produced by particular groups will be identified and categorized in terms of the type of literature they represent and the interpretive function they perform as a finished product.

SCRIPTURAL DIALOGUE IN THE WRITINGS

From these three foci—explicit references, interpretations, and the resultant shape—conclusions may be drawn about the extent and scope of Torah and Prophets as the primary scripture for the formative period of post-exilic Judaism. This can be done only after all of the literature of the Writings is examined. In addition to these observations, however, further conclusions will be drawn concerning the dialogue within the Writings themselves. Because this literature was produced at a time when there was yet no final consensus about what scripture is or how it should be used, we should expect to find dialogue among the various interpretive alternatives espoused. Such a dialogue helps us to understand more clearly the nature of the post-exilic period. It also points to different interpretive stances: some were normative and primary, and others were optional and secondary. All of these perspectives and interpretations found within the Writings became canonical and, therefore, normative for Judaism and Christianity. The dialogue within the Writings contains clues and keys to the ways in which future communities will view and use both this literature and the authoritative literature to which they respond and point.

The primary attention of this chapter is on the *texts* of the Writings. Although our examination of this literature is based upon the community divisions discussed above (sages, psalmists, community builders, visionaries, and storytellers), this chapter focuses on the types of literature produced by these groups. Such a focus facilitates a transition into the subsequent history of Judaism and emergent Christianity from which we can trace the continuity, or discontinuity, between the types of textual interpretation begun in the literature of the Writings (chapter 5). Such a focus also prepares the way for a discussion of the canonical shape and function of this literature (chapter 6). Interpretive communities with their new needs and crises come and go; the texts they produce and the hermeneutical options they provide sometimes long outlive them. Such is the case for the post-exilic Writings, and this is the reason we now turn our attention to these *texts*.

The purpose and format of this chapter rest upon certain presuppositions central to our arguments about the nature of a scriptural community in general and post-exilic Israel in particular. Pivotal for the hermeneutics of scriptural communities is a dialogue between text and community (chapter 2). This dialogue involves a twofold shaping process. First, the "new" developments in the life of a community create the need for new interpretations and applications of the old authoritative texts. Chapter 3 had as one of its primary purposes the explication of such needs and the identification of those groups within each community who sought to provide new interpretations. Second, the old helps to shape the new. This observation provides the rationale for the present chapter and its focus on the text. The concern is to answer the question, not of why a particular interpretation is given (for this question is already partially answered), but of what is being interpreted and how. The literature of the Writings, although reflecting new methods and new crises, is also controlled by and must be seen in relationship with the old texts now central to all of Israel.

Sometimes, as we have seen in the literature of the sages and the storytellers, explicit references to an authoritative text may be difficult to find. Nevertheless, the overall function and role of such literature is examined in light of the fundamental dialogue presupposed. A thesis of this study is that explicit references to scripture need not be the only or primary mark of a scriptural community. Rather, the particular needs of such communities, although motivated by and presupposing such a dialogue, may result in writings more focused on the hoped-for results of such a dialogue (e.g., faithful living) than on the identification and affirmation of a central text itself.

Because hermeneutics begin with the community, chapter 3 was an essential first step in our discussion. It is now necessary to examine the basic texts of post-exilic Israel so that a fuller and more complete picture of the hermeneutics of post-exilic Israel can be given. The thesis that Torah and Prophets were authoritative and central will be tested. In doing so, we will find that some of the Writings themselves are becoming authoritative; that is, the interpretations of some post-exilic communities are gradually becoming normative for all of Judaism, while others remain as footnotes or minority reports. If we are to understand the future development of Jewish and Christian scriptural interpretation, we must pay attention to this phenomenon within the scriptural dialogue as well.

The setting for our analysis of Torah, Prophets, and the Writings remains the post-exilic period of Israel. Diversity, lack of consensus, no final canon—this characterizes and qualifies our conclusions in this chapter. I have maintained that Torah and Prophets are becoming the central authoritative textual tradition and that this is one ingredient of whatever it means to speak of God, Israel, mission, and identity. If this is correct, then the texts of the Writings should reflect it.

SAPIENTIAL LITERATURE

Discussing the relationship of wisdom literature to Torah and Prophets has always been a difficult task for historians, students of literature, and theologians: the social locus and provenance of the wisdom tradition, the very different ways in which the sages formulated their message, the focus on human experience versus revelation, and the quite different, even contradictory theological perspectives in Proverbs, Job, and Ecclesiastes represent challenges. Nevertheless, a few clear references to and uses of Torah and Prophets in this literature have significant import for our understanding of the sages in the post-exilic period.

There are at least three types of explicit uses of Torah in sapiential literature. First, a concern with creation is shared by both (e.g., Prov. 8:22–31; Job 28:20–28). Whether or not creation is to be seen as a late and secondary development within Torah, with its inclusion perhaps even motivated by sapiential thought, is of little importance here. Rather, the affirmation that God is creator of the world in sapiential literature ties its concerns to those now important affirmations in Torah and the Prophets (e.g., Genesis 1; Isa. 51:12–16). A second, central concern of this literature with education is directly related to similar emphases in Torah (e.g., Deut. 6:20–25) and highlights a critical function of scripture as the repository of values and traditions essential for the understanding of what it means to be the people of God. Finally, although it makes no explicit references to particular Torah texts, sapiential literature is concerned with the acts of faithful cultic life, namely, sacrifice, vows, and prayer.[1] Such concerns in post-exilic literature would inevitably be related to the source that mandates and explicates such activities: Torah.

The explicit influence of Prophets is also found in sapiential literature. The connection of Proverbs and Ecclesiastes to Solomon (and, perhaps, also to the Song of Solomon) is significant. Not only does such an association call to mind the stories of Solomon (and others, such as Hezekiah) in the Former Prophets; more important, it also affirms and continues to validate the authoritative role of this kind of teacher and sage. Such a function is important not only for the Former Prophets but also for other literature in the Writings (2 Chronicles) and beyond (e.g., Wisdom of Solomon). The picture of wisdom as a prophetess (Prov. 1:20 ff.) also represents an important connection between sapiential literature and the Prophets. The call to obedience and knowledge not only represents a dialogue with the prophetic functions but also paves the way for other and different calls and visions of sage types such as Daniel. Finally, in the books of Ecclesiastes and Job we find debates and discussions about eschatology and the end of life (e.g., Eccles. 3:16–22, Job 14) that are to be related to similar if differently conceived concerns in the Prophets.

Although all of the examples cited above represent important connections between sapiential literature and Torah-Prophets, it must be acknowledged that the basic literary forms (*meshalim*, dialogue, long poems on wisdom, and so forth) and the reason-oriented, experientially based wisdom teachings reflect a quite different way of viewing the world and God from those found in Torah and Prophets. Still, there are at least two important and related connections between Torah-Prophets and wisdom: retribution and theodicy. Regardless of different theological presuppositions, the two-ways (good-bad) system of the sages and the retributional perspective of, for example, Deuteronomic theology are functioning in similar ways. Both systems evaluate the present actions of individuals in light of a God-given order and intention in this world and make appropriate judgments, admonitions, and predictions. Although the final literary picture created by the Deuteronomistic History begins with the law of Moses (analogous to the created order presupposed by the sages), it seems clear that the real hermeneutical starting point is the contemporary misfortune of Israel. Both the sages and Torah-Prophets begin with experience and seek to understand the subsequent actions of God in light of this and in light of similar theological intentions. The problem of theodicy, an important problem for the sages, is in part occasioned by the conflict between a Torah-Prophets worldview and the present plight of post-exilic (or exilic) Israel.

The result of this sometimes oblique but nevertheless very present dialogue between the worldview of the sages and Torah-Prophets is a sapiential literature that is often seen in opposition to a revelation-centered cultic religion. Although we should not underestimate the differences, such a polarizing perspective, especially within the context of post-exilic Israel, is unfortunate. It is perhaps more the product of contemporary dichotomies—between reason and revelation or between natural and revealed religion—than differences found in this particular period. The authoritative texts of Torah and Prophets provide important values and directions for post-exilic Israel and its life as the people of God. Through theological perspectives that are compatible, if not identical, to Torah-Prophets, the sages address the problems of living in their time through their own particular literary ways. Drawing upon a basic belief in the goodness of the created order, this literature complements and intensifies a concern to learn from the experiences of the past. Most of this literature is inherently conservative and, as such, rests upon the same concerns as the Torah-Prophets and much of the Writings to establish and maintain community. Such goals and concerns readily explain both the editorial activity of the sages in Torah and Prophets (e.g., Hos. 14:9) and the ultimate connections that will be made between wisdom as the goal of the sage and Torah as the central authoritative text of Israel (e.g., Ecclus. 24:23). In all probability, such a connection and perceived compatibility between wisdom and Torah is not only or even primarily the result of post-exilic Judaism; it is reflective of a basic connection and interrelationship present from the earliest times of Israel's life.[2]

LITURGICAL LITERATURE

The Psalms more than any other literature in the Writings reflect an explicit use of virtually every major tradition in Torah. All of the Torah "story"—creation, patriarchs, Moses, the exodus, the wilderness, wandering, Sinai, the law—and the major themes contained within it are used by the Psalms. They also make use of the stories of monarchical Israel and Judah up to and including the fall of Jerusalem and its aftermath in the post-exilic period, meaning they depend upon the Former Prophets and perhaps Ezra–Nehemiah as well. The significant role of David as singer, composer, and collector also represents a use of this authoritative literature and is analogous with the role of Solomon in sapiential literature. The importance of the Prophets for this liturgical literature is witnessed to by the so-called prophetic psalms (e.g., 85:8–13 and 95:7–11), where prophetic oracles are uttered by cultic leaders within the context of worship. Because many of the psalms are composed in the post-exilic period, a dialogue between liturgical literature and other developments found within the rest of the Writings is also present. Wisdom psalms, Torah psalms, the collection of psalms by temple groups organized and authorized in this period, and the presence of many Diaspora psalms in both Psalms and Lamentations reflect this dialogue.

Unlike wisdom literature, where we must search hard to find a few examples of the explicit use of an authoritative scripture, the Psalms and Lamentations present an embarrassment of riches. In doing so, they not only point to the needs of post-exilic Israel and all of its communities but also represent an essential component of the literature itself: the integration of old (authoritative text) and new (new stories, new experiences) within the worship of God as absolutely essential for continuance of the relationship between God and people.

The liturgical literature makes use of the authoritative texts so central to their content in many ways. All of these must be related to the context of worship and meditation in a way that provides the rationale for their composition and collection into a corpus. The Psalms have been called the prayerbook and the songbook of ancient Israel; both designations contain important clues to their character and function. On the one hand, this literature is most often prayer, words of the people directed to God for the purposes of petition, complaint or lament, vow, trust, praise, and so forth. Each of these purposes is associated with the particular literary form that accomplishes its goals. On the other hand, the modes of prayer are varied, although perhaps the most common means in the Psalms is singing in joy, in despair, or in an admixture of both.

The purposes and modes of liturgical literature are related to a great number of occasions when prayer and song are seen to be appropriate.

Although the general activity of worship is certainly occasion enough for singing and praying, this literature reflects other special occasions (e.g., pilgrimage, feast days, weddings, enthronements) when thanksgiving, lamentation, and confession are appropriate. In all of this, the world of the people is brought into dialogue with the authoritative texts. These texts challenge, remind, and direct the people to relate their present and future to the past. At least half the time in the Psalms, this dialogue results in lamentation, for the promises of life and prosperity when the people are in right relationship with God are not always readily being fulfilled. In times of both adversity and prosperity, the theological values and systems found with Torah and Prophets are used both to explain present suffering or success and to call the people to repentance or thanksgiving. Torah and Prophets thus represent an important element in the Psalms, providing in part the rationale for and the shape of the liturgical forms in which this literature is manifested.

The overall result of this hermeneutical activity is a collection of prayers, songs, and meditations that continually relate Torah and Prophets to the present life of the people. The wonder of this literature lies not in its particular theological visions but rather in its ability to transcend the particular occasions and purposes for which it was "originally" composed. Somehow the larger purposes of praise, lament, and confession, so essential for the continuance of a relationship with God, allow this literature to be reused for new occasions and new challenges that differ from their initial settings. In this way the old texts of Israel are always new in the life of the people. Thus, royal monarchical psalms may speak in new, eschatological ways to a post-exilic Israel with no king. Or, a catechetical psalm originally associated with temple entrance may be used when the Temple is in ruins. Or, a theodicy psalm may transcend the particular worship setting of its composer and speak to all who have ever anguished over the success of the wicked.

In other words, this literature, so important to Christians and Jews at all times, witnesses to the vital task of relating the authoritative texts of the community to the present day. Those texts, referred to and used in all types of different prayer forms, are constantly reactualized in light of the continual needs of confession, trust, lament, and praise. Although such a process began long before the books of Psalms and Lamentations were collected and put in their final form, in post-exilic Israel are found the particular texts to be used and the particular collection that would become authoritative for all subsequent communities. Surely post-exilic Judaism continued to write new psalms and compose new prayers. The Psalms are an essential paradigm, both directing and legitimating this ongoing activity.

HISTORICAL LITERATURE

The historical literature reflects much knowledge of the content of Torah and Prophets. First Chronicles, beginning with a patrilineal genealogy, makes use of materials in Torah to trace a history from Adam to Zedakiah. Of particular importance in this genealogy is the Davidic line (Former Prophets) as well as the Levites and the sons of Aaron (Torah). A concern with priestly families (15:4), the patriarchs (12:17; 16:8ff.; 28:8), and Moses (6:1–19; 15:5; 21:29) all function to ground the present history in the Torah story. However, the overwhelming focus of 1 Chronicles is upon David and results in a much heavier use of the traditions found in the Prophets. David, rather than Moses or Aaron, is the one who established the cult as we now know it. David is in charge of the service of song (6:31–48), commands the Levites to appoint singers (15:16), appoints them as ministers, and organizes the sacrificial cult (23:26ff.). David ultimately looks much like Moses: As Moses cannot go into the promised land, so David may not build the Temple. Solomon—like Moses' Joshua—is ready to continue and complete the work David has begun. In both cases, however, Moses and David provide blueprints for their successors, for living the law and building the temple, respectively.

Second Chronicles presents a picture of the history from Solomon to Cyrus grounded in the regulations and priorities of the Torah. On the one hand, the tent of meeting (1:3), the ark of the covenant (5:7), the tables of the law (5:10), the statutes and ordinances (7:18), the law and commandments of Moses (8:13; 24:6; 25:4; 30:16; 35:12), and many other references tie the monarchical history to Torah. On the other hand, David is the paradigm for the manner in which future kings are to act and the cult is to be organized. Although the origin of future-shaping statutes, ordinances, and other priorities are to be found in Torah, David who acts in accordance with them becomes the reference point and the authoritative yardstick for community organization and direction.

The Book of Ezra begins with a reference to the prophetic hope for restoration centered in Jerusalem. The function of David as critical to the organization of the cult (3:10; 5:11; 8:20) is assumed but is not of primary importance to this book. Moses and the written law associated with him (3:2; 6:18; 7:6) are referred to much more frequently than David. A concern to relate the present practices of the community to the traditions and stories of the law results in a significantly larger number of references to Torah material than to Prophets (3:4; 6:19; 7:5, 10–11; 9:1, 7; 10:3). This emphasis continues in the Book of Nehemiah. Moses and the law (1:7f.; 8:1, 13, 14, 18; 9:3; 10:28ff.) are appropriate examples. Throughout all of this, however, the city of David (3:16; 12:37), with all of the prophetic overtones elicited by such references, provides a rationale for the locus of the reforms of Ezra and Nehemiah. These Davidic traditions also create a significant historical continuum between Moses and the law and the post-exilic Jerusalem community.

In summarizing the references to Torah and Prophets, it is not surprising to find more references to the Prophets in 1–2 Chronicles, for this represents a retelling of the Deuteronomistic History as found in the Former Prophets. Nevertheless, this literature is grounded in the Torah story, even though the focus is more upon Moses as he appears as a prophet and as the recipient of the Word of God than upon the law itself. The parallels we have suggested between Moses and David and between their successors, Joshua and Solomon, can be extended one step further if Ezra and Nehemiah are included. Ezra assumes the roles of Moses and David, to establish the community through special sources of revelation, whereas Nehemiah assumes the roles of Joshua and Solomon, to carry out the work begun by his predecessor.[3]

In 2 Chronicles Moses appears to be given a more authoritative role. There is a special concern to make the authority of David contingent upon and in line with a Mosaic legal tradition. David is still the most central figure for this history, as the architect of the cult and as a prophet whose words and deeds have import for the future life of the community. The history ends with a reference to Jeremiah's prediction of restoration, reflecting again the importance of the Prophets in its shaping.

Ezra–Nehemiah continue to demonstrate the importance of Prophets for understanding community. The prophecy-fulfillment schema that begins Ezra and the references to David and Jerusalem affirm the centrality of this particular community for Judaism as envisioned in the Prophets. Yet it is dependent upon a Torah picture that sees the post-exilic community of Jerusalem as an outgrowth of the stories and promises contained within it. Thus, although the Prophets are important for certain details and for a carrying of the promises, Torah is primary. Over and over again, what the community does now is explained and justified in terms of its necessary congruence with the old, with the law of Moses. Whether a building project, the divisions of the priests, the festal calendar, or the interpretation of the law—all of this is related to the law. The living out of legal obligation in the context of a covenantal relationship is set forth as the primary goal and mission of the people of God.

The result of the hermeneutical activity represented by the historical literature in the Writings seems at first to provide Judaism with a new version of the Former Prophets and a history of the early post-exilic period. However, when these writings were juxtaposed to Torah and Prophets, which continue to be central and authoritative, a different picture of their function is achieved. The midrashic character of 1–2 Chronicles is clear. This "history" is not intended to replace its analogue and source, the Former Prophets. Rather, its particular emphasis on and interpretation of Torah and Prophets are intended to highlight those aspects of the old story, now retold, that are essential for contemporary communities to use. As such, this history is an interpretive lens through which we must look if we are to understand the pertinence and applicability of the past. More important, perhaps, 1–2 Chronicles represents paradigmatically a process, the rereading and reinterpretation of the story for present communities, in which all subsequent communities must engage.

Similarly, the primary value of Ezra–Nehemiah is not to be found in the history it presents. Rather, the roles of Ezra and Nehemiah as Torah-centered leaders, obedient and committed to the values of the authoritative texts of the community, are crucial to the purpose of this literature. In this sense, this literature is more concerned to present a biblical ethics than a history of the post-exilic period.

Viewed as a whole, the historical literature reflects a need for paradigms of behavior and a presentation of the past and present to be thoroughly integrated into the values and stories of authoritative scripture, Torah-Prophets. Without such scripture these books lose their source and their purpose. Although, as with sapiential and liturgical literature, important antecedents exist in pre-exilic biblical literature for the retelling of ancient stories and the creation of new ones, the fixed and central role of Torah and Prophets in the post-exilic period makes the nature and function of these texts new.

APOCALYPTIC LITERATURE

Much apocalyptic literature is associated with more central biblical figures than Daniel. Moreover, this book contains relatively few direct references or allusions to Torah and Prophets. Nevertheless, Daniel is wholly unintelligible in terms of its function and message without the presupposition of a dialogue between the community that produced it and the authoritative texts of Torah and Prophets.

The portrait of Daniel as a sage and royal interpreter of dreams has often been paralleled with the story of Joseph. Comparisons with this Torah story and its provenance in wisdom circles seem apt. Such comparisons with authoritative figures in Torah would serve to validate the picture of Daniel. The behavior of Daniel in observing the laws and customs of Judaism grounded in Torah as well as the prayer of confession in chapter 9 (note the parallels with Nehemiah, references to the law of Moses and a retributional theology, the prophets, etc.) also reflects a knowledge and use of Torah.

The influence of the Prophets is also pervasive in this book. The symbolism of the tree (4:10, 22), the eschatological framework, and the receipt of visions—all of this rests upon pictures of these prophets and their particular messages. The prophecy originally found in Jer. 25:11 (29:10) and explicated in Dan. 9:24–27 is a very good example of midrashic exegesis. This prophecy had already been subject to interpretation (e.g., 2 Chron. 36:22; Ezra 1:1). Here, an authoritative text from the Prophets is subjected to an interpretation in Daniel that attempts to explain the apparent delay of its fulfillment by suggesting seventy years refers to seventy weeks of years. We can find no better example of the interaction between authoritative text and the needs of a scriptural community than this particular text.

In its final form, the Book of Daniel represents a clear response to Torah and Prophets in light of the needs of a particular and oppressed community. The connection of Torah and Prophets with a scribal tradition is clear. The need to express new revelations in forms with scriptural precedent is equally clear. The figure of the seer-sage, Daniel, as the appropriate vehicle for such new revelation draws upon two distinct but interrelated developments. On the one hand, Daniel, through his name and actions, stands with Joseph and the prophets. On the other hand, Daniel as a sage represents the authoritative post-exilic scribal tradition through which the meaning of Torah and Prophets is made available. Thus, the Book of Daniel points backward to the basic scriptures, Torah and Prophets, and forward to the ongoing process of interpretation to which these scriptures must be subject if they are to provide direction for the present.

The uses made of scripture in Daniel are similar to those found within the sapiential, liturgical, and historical literature of the Writings.

A relatively unknown (if known at all; cf., Ezek. 14:14) figure is made authoritative through parallels with another biblical hero and his obedience to the religious traditions of Torah. A prominent and oft-cited prophecy is reinterpreted to make it applicable to the present situation of the community. In both of these cases, the authority and relevance of Torah and Prophets are witnessed to by the visionaries.

The use of Torah and Prophets in apocalyptic literature results in new visions—in a literature that has a new form and message for the elect. However, the figure of David, at once a sage, a prophet, and a follower of Torah, depends upon all of these for the legitimation and validation of his new message. Surely we must recognize the newness of the apocalyptic vision, but we must also take seriously the authoritative texts upon which such a picture of Daniel and his message stand. The overall purpose of this literature is not to replace Torah or the Prophets but rather to explain their pertinence and even to encourage obedience based upon them in very adverse conditions. The desperate situation requires new visions and new literature. Yet, such literature is only valid if it is seen as continuous within the values of Torah and Prophets and in dialogue with the story of Israel found therein.

EDIFYING LITERATURE

As has already been noted, the Books of Ruth and Esther do not contain large numbers of citations from Torah and Prophets. Although enough evidence is present to suggest that Torah and Prophets were functioning authoritatively for these books, the relative paucity of scriptural citations perhaps indicates a different function for this edifying literature. In order to understand this function and the special role this literature has within the Writings, we will need to examine the interrelationship of these books not only with Torah and Prophets but with the Writings as well.

The multivalence of the Book of Ruth—the fact that this story can and has been associated with many different settings—should serve as a warning against a simplistic discussion of its use and its dependence upon particular scriptural passages and messages. For example, although the literary setting of the judges might suggest the knowledge and use of the Deuteronomistic Book of Judges, the anti-Moabite bias of this literature (e.g., Deut. 23:4ff.) makes such a conclusion difficult. Again, although comparisons may be drawn between the legal questions, regulations, and procedures concerning marriage into a father's family, the next of kin, or rights of inheritance, a close examination of the Book of Ruth suggests that the author has created a different picture with different purposes that may have little or no concern to provide commentary on Torah regulations and procedures. Although parallels between the genealogy in 4:18–22 and 1 Chron. 2:9–15 suggest an interrelationship, it is far from certain how Ruth as a book intends to use this material.

In spite of these difficulties, the preceding examples represent places where the post-exilic community, cognizant of Torah and Prophets, would have found parallels or would have called to mind authoritative literature with similar content, if quite different purposes. The setting of Bethlehem, the time "when judges ruled," as well as the concluding genealogies, are to be related to the Former Prophets. The legal concerns over inheritance and next of kin, the role of the heroine, and the concern with Moab would all have been juxtaposed to stories and laws within Torah.

The Book of Ruth represents an interpretation and use of Torah and Prophets that, on the one hand, stand firmly within the traditions and norms of this scripture. A concern to glorify the place of David, to present a picture of a faithful heroine who obtains, much like Jacob, her rightful inheritance according to the "laws" of the community, albeit by some devious behavior, is a picture of scriptural piety with much precedent. On the other hand, the Moabite ancestry of Ruth and the inclusive portrait of the people of Israel presented goes against the grain of much post-exilic thought. Yet, both of these messages of Ruth as a book are to be found in Torah and Prophets. Such a message, combining traditions and scriptural concerns used by others in this period for quite different purposes, is testimony to the scriptural pluralism possible at the time.

In Esther, there are many places that depend upon a knowledge of texts in Torah and Prophets and several others that are enhanced by a comparison. The wisdom motifs of the story, the court setting, the bestowal of royal honors (e.g., robes) upon the wise—all of these recall the similar story of Joseph. Very striking is the picture of Mordecai as second in power to the king and as champion of the Jewish people, a picture very similar to that of Joseph in Genesis.

Perhaps the most important use of Torah and Prophets is that presupposed by the action of Mordecai in refusing to bow down to Haman. This refusal is grounded in both Torah and Prophets. The conflict between Mordecai, a Benjaminite, and Haman, an Agagite, is paralleled by the conflict between Saul and Agag in 1 Sam. 15:7–9. The conflict in the Former Prophets is itself based upon a Torah history of trouble and conflict with the Amalekites and upon the explicit injunction to destroy Amalek in Deut. 25:17–19. With the explicit reference to Mordecai as a Benjaminite (2:5), the use of the Torah and Prophets to explain the subsequent conflict seems clear. Because this conflict results in the threat to all Jews and in the feast of Purim, such use of scripture is of central importance for the entire book.

The second letter concerning Purim (9:29–32) is usually seen as reflecting the need for a literary record of the feast in light of its absence in Torah lists of feasts. However, this text may also use the Prophets as a further way of legitimatizing the feast. The phrase "peace and truth" (9:30) is sometimes related to Zech. 8:19 and its description of other post-exilic ritual occasions.

In addition to these references, the penitence (4:1) and mourning (6:12) of Mordecai can be related to scriptural traditions, although an intentional reference to them is questionable. Further, the parallels with the Book of Daniel (court setting, wisdom emphasis, threat to Jews) as well as the presence of the name Mordecai on the list of returning exiles in Ezra 2:2 (Neh. 7:7) serve to connect this book with literature in the Writings as well.

The first observation to be made about these two stories is that they do not represent a consensus view. Although Ruth functions at one level to glorify David, this is surely not the primary purpose of the story as a whole. Both Ruth and Esther set forth particular commentaries on the nature and function of community. These commentaries, although related to traditions found within Torah and Prophets, provide special insight when seen in dialogue with the notions of community found particularly in 1–2 Chronicles and Ezra–Nehemiah. From a social and historical perspective, such an observation may point toward a growing consensus about Judaism controlled by the adherents of this historical literature, although the very existence of Ruth and Esther suggests there is still more to be said and done. At the literary level, however, it may be suggested this edifying literature represents another level within the Writings, namely, literature that has its rhyme and reason not only as it relates to Torah and Prophets but also as it relates to a growing body of non-Torah and non-Prophets literature (i.e., the Writings). Although there is no reason to assume all types of edifying literature have this function and place within the overall framework of Torah, Prophets, and Writings, there seems to be enough evidence to suggest this is the case for Ruth and Esther. Perhaps the Song of Solomon finds its most comfortable placement and function within the Writings in this way as well. In that case, however, the literature it appears to comment upon or is to be seen in relationship with is sapiential.

CONCLUSIONS

On the basis of this overview of the literature of the Writings and its use of Torah and Prophets, a few conclusions may be drawn. Relying upon either direct citation or very clear allusions and parallels (see Chart 1), the Writings when viewed as a whole clearly reflect the fact that the texts of Torah and Prophets were widely known and used by all the communities represented in this literature. Such an observation does not permit us to assume a "canon" in the post-exilic period, but it does point toward a growing consensus that these texts are central to all. Clearly, this consensus is a necessary prerequisite for the final determination of what will be in or out of the canon at a later period.

When the hermeneutics used by the Writings in their use of Torah and Prophets are surveyed, we are unable to find one particular approach to Torah and Prophets that is shared by all and able to win the day. All post-exilic communities are concerned to determine how best to live faithfully in difficult times, but such a common goal does not suggest one way to view Torah and Prophets theologically, socially, or otherwise. Yet, all these textual traditions take the authority of the central texts seriously. In the final analysis, when viewed *together*, it is only this that the Writings share.

Perhaps the most common feature of post-exilic hermeneutics in the Writings is the use of figures (Ezra, Nehemiah, Ruth, Esther, Daniel, Solomon, and so forth) either who are to be located in the past (Torah and Prophets) or who find their authority on the basis of parallels with these past figures. Of course, this can be debated because the ways in which such past figures are used differ greatly.

The result of all the hermeneutical activity in the post-exilic period is a body of different types of literature, each with its own particular focus and each with its own way of making Torah and Prophets applicable to the life of their communities. Such an observation is merely the other side of our conclusions about community at that time, namely, that different communities (or different groups within the same community) produce different texts. Nevertheless, these texts and the hermeneutics associated with them gradually become the property of all post-exilic Judaism and present biblical communities with a variety of ways to interpret and use their book.

Chart 1.

Torah and Prophets in the Writings

	Sapiential	Liturgical	Historical	Apocalyptic	Edifying	
Genesis 1—11 (Creation)	X	X	X			Torah
Genesis 12—50 (Patriarchs)		X	X	X	X	
Exodus 1—18 (Exodus and Wanderings)		X	X			
Exodus 19–Numbers (Sinai)	X	X	X	X	X	
Deuteronomy	X	X	X			
Former Prophets	X	X	X		X	Prophets
Latter Prophets	X	X	X	X		

This development is authenticated within the Writings themselves (Chart 2). With the exception of a questionable relationship between edifying and apocalyptic literature (and probably the Song of Solomon), there appears to be a dialogue between all other types of literature found in the Writings and the communities that produced them. This suggests that sapiential, liturgical, historical, and apocalyptic literature

Chart 2.

Dialogue within the Writings

	Sapiential	Liturgical	Historical	Apocalyptic	Edifying
Sapiential	-	X	X	X	X
Liturgical	X	-	X	X	X
Historical	X	X	-	X	X
Apocalyptic	X	X	X	-	?
Edifying	X	X	X	?	-

may all be seen as legitimate ways to interpret Torah and Prophets and that such approaches have become widespread in post-exilic Judaism.

This is not to suggest, however, that Ruth and Esther are illegitimate. Rather, their tangential relationship to Torah and Prophets and their lack of dialogue with each other indicate a more localized use of these stories. Such use may also, as we have noted above, place this literature in a special category within the Writings themselves, namely, as responses to the Writings rather than to Torah and Prophets. Although the subsequent flowering of apocalyptic literature may argue against this, the ambiguous relationship of Ruth and Esther to Daniel may point to a similar status for apocalyptic literature; that is, although both edifying and apocalyptic literature are clearly related to all other types of literature in the Writings, the fact that they do not seem to have much relationship to each other may indicate that both types of literature are, at this point in the history of the post-exilic period, minority reports used only by small communities with special needs or concerns. This view of apocalyptic is compatible with contemporary sociological and theological studies of the literature. However, to draw this conclusion in light of the proliferation of apocalyptic literature in Judaism and Christianity brings with it the necessary assumption that such a minority report form (i.e., the apocalypse) will become a very common way for many different minorities to express themselves. This literature may then become a way to differentiate and separate, rather than to draw together.

There are several different ways to explain the hermeneutical activity and its results that we have described in the Writings. Surely, the development of a growing textual body of literature is central to any thesis. The texts are becoming fixed, at least within particular communities, and the implications are great. To cite but one example: "Prophets" are no longer simply or primarily individuals; they are books to be read and studied. The figure of Daniel who interprets as a sage-seer the text of Jeremiah is dependent upon such a development. However, it is not simply the Prophets who become "books," it is Torah and the Writings as well. The character of the Writings is referential, and the reference is not to an oral tradition but rather to a fixed literary tradition.

All of this development can and has been studied by historians of tradition and Israelite religion. For example, to observe that wisdom thought becomes prominent after prophecy ceases,[4] that visionaries carry on the prophetic tradition, or that Ezra and Nehemiah represent a consensus view of Judaism—all of these conclusions may be made to explain the phenomenon we have traced and to place it within a larger framework. The use of theological, sociological, literary, and historical perspectives are all important in our quest to understand and explain. Unfortunately, most developmental perspectives are necessarily affected by the same hermeneutical characteristic we find in all interpretations, whether or not it is acknowledged. Namely, they begin with a view of Israel or Judaism that is found not within the texts but rather within their contemporary communities. Such perspectives inevitably affect the view of the Torah, Prophets, or the Writings.

Although the present study does not claim to be free of such hermeneutical constraints, it does wish to err on a more conservative side in drawing developmental conclusions. Thus, we will not suggest which of the hermeneutical stances in the Writings is most important. Torah is becoming central, with the Prophets not far behind. The sage is becoming a critically important figure for biblical interpretation, as witnessed to by wisdom literature and the evidence of sapiential thought and editorial activity in Torah, Prophets, and Writings. That the Writings are to be understood in terms of their relationship first to Torah and Prophets and second to each other also seems clear. However, the implications of such a literary and social phenomenon for canon must await further discussion.

The dialogue between community and text appears to explain best the Writings and their function within post-exilic Israel. Nevertheless, this literature, although focused on an increasingly fixed and authoritative textual tradition, does not yet suggest a consensus about biblical interpretation. Rather, it points to an ongoing activity of interpretation between many different communities and an authoritative text. Sometimes there is dialogue between these communities, sometimes not. Yet, the way is paved for more "writings," and it is to this development that we now turn.

5

Continuity of the
Scriptural Pattern

By the end of the third century B.C.E. there is ample testimony to the existence of Torah and Prophets as a scripture for all Jewish communities. Moreover, although several of the Writings utilize prophetic concerns and messages, the authority of the Prophets is tied directly to Torah, which is becoming the point of departure for interpretation by all Jewish scriptural communities. However, as we have seen, the combining, or marriage, of Torah and Prophets creates a tension concerning the way in which God's will is to be made manifest in the life of the community. Despite the attempts of one group or another to resolve this tension, it remains.

INTERTESTAMENTAL LITERATURE, THE NEW TESTAMENT, AND RABBINIC LITERATURE

A multifaceted concept of pluralism is essential for understanding and explaining the form and function of the Writings in the post-exilic period. From the period of the exile to the present day, Judaism and Christianity have been characterized by cultural pluralism. Such a pluralism is almost by definition necessary to explain a Diaspora religion. In addition, the nature of Torah and Prophets represents a scriptural pluralism: a message capable of many different interpretations and applications. The demonstration of this is the Writings.

Nevertheless, it appears inappropriate to characterize the authors of the Writings as pluralists. Because this literature reflects many particular ways of interpreting and living Torah and Prophets, it is better to envision several different groups utilizing scripture, sometimes in interrelated ways, to set forth their particular agendas as proposals they would like the majority to adopt. So, for example, the centrality of Jerusalem is the hope of some, but not all. Again, Torah becomes authoritative for all Jews, but how it should be interpreted, and by whom, is a matter of much debate. Even if we accept the view that the sage-scribe is the major authority figure for many scriptural communities, we have seen that the interests and concerns of these figures are not homogeneous. In all probability, although there is some indication that diverse groups and communities were coexisting, even working together, with a common scripture, the Writings themselves, as a pluralistic response to Torah and Prophets, are best viewed as representing a later, literary, pluralism found in the canon but not necessarily in the post-exilic period.

Yet, a few comments are in order. Although the pluralism of the Writings may be an artificial (but not superficial) construct, the pluralism of Torah and Prophets is not. The nature of social and political community life may result in one-sided approaches or evaluations of what is central to Israel, but the fact that there are responses to Torah and Prophets as diverse as those found within the Writings is symptomatic of a diversity contained not simply in different post-exilic communities and their needs but also, more importantly for our purposes, within scripture itself.

The Writings—in their diversity, if not in their witness to historical pluralism—remind us of this scriptural pluralism in Torah and Prophets. If we view the Writings solely in a historical and developmental manner, they point us toward an ever increasing centrality of Torah and the control of the sages over its interpretation. That this conclusion is the consensus of current scholarship is exemplified in the following statements.

> In this new modality as a community patterning its life on Torah, and concerned with the faithful application of that norm to every detail of life, the new scribe class came to assume a position rivaling the priesthood over the course of the fourth and third centuries B.C.E. It is safe to say that, in everyday matters, the scribe exercised the greater influence over the life of the individual Jew.[1]

> The Torah was the basic component in the tradition and those who would remain within Judaism had to relate themselves to it in some way.[2]

> . . . in times as chaotic and threatening to Jewish existence as those of the late Hellenistic and early Roman periods, the efforts to demonstrate that in spite of appearances all life fit into the pattern of meaning revealed in the Torah, became an urgent necessity.[3]

Surely, the Writings confirm such views. Yet, they *also* demonstrate that "a number of different approaches could be taken within the parameters of the tradition."[4]

In summary, by the time the Writings are complete, we can see a cultural pluralism created by the Diaspora and a scriptural pluralism created by Torah and Prophets. The Writings are influenced by both cultural and scriptural pluralism, although *viewed individually* and historically they reflect several nonpluralistic responses to scripture and to culture. When *viewed as a totality,* however, they witness to a growing consensus about the centrality of Torah and may function as a prism to demonstrate the many different ways to be a scriptural community, to make sense of the world we live in, and to relate that world to the stories and stipulations of old.

Although understanding the historical setting and message of the Writings is important, the diversity this literature represents when viewed as a whole is the critical factor for understanding the subsequent history of Judaism and Christianity. The history of Judaism and Christianity from the late Hellenistic and early Roman periods (ca. 200 B.C.E.) to the time of the formation of the New Testament and the Mishnah (ca. 200 C.E.) is a period filled with upheaval, with persecution, and conflict. One recent commentator has characterized the effects of this period as follows.

> Alongside those who remained dedicated to a community centered around the temple cult and the concept of the eternal Torah as interpreted by the scribes, there arose others who, while also dedicated to lives of obedience to the Torah, interpreted the scriptural tradition with far greater dependence on prophetic and apocalyptic themes. . . . they called into question current temple practices, challenged the authority of the presiding priests . . .[5]

At least one of the books in the Writings, Daniel, represents a response to such conditions. We have noted that Daniel reflects both the stability of Torah and the sage-seer, as well as an apocalyptic worldview at some variance with a consensus view about the nature of a Torah community as found in, for example, Ezra and Nehemiah.

Precisely here—in their witness both to the stability and consensus of scripture and to the diversity of interpretation possible and necessary in light of radically different circumstances—the Writings represent a critical source for understanding the future of Judaism. The period from 200 B.C.E. to 200 C.E. generated an enormous amount of literature. This literature, found in the Apocrypha, the Pseudepigrapha, the Qumran writings, the New Testament, and early rabbinic traditions, contains many different literary forms and messages coming from all parts of the ancient Near East. Yet, most of this literature, Jewish in origin, is intentionally and explicitly related to scripture—usually Torah and Prophets, sometimes the Writings. This literature often has been used to paint a picture of a radically sectarian Judaism. However, recent scholarship has warned us against too easily assuming a diversity within the nature of the Judaism of this period.

> Speculative difference on the time and nature of the end are not . . . constitutive of different types or patterns of religion.[6]

> While it is now recognized that foreign ideas penetrated deep into many aspects of Jewish thought, and that sometimes it is difficult to decide whether an early document is essentially Jewish or Christian, it is, nevertheless, unwise to exaggerate the diversity in early Judaism. In the first century Judaism was neither uniformly normative nor chaotically diverse.[7]

The Writings—in their witness both to a consensus about the form and content of Torah and Prophets and to a diversity of interpretation—are the precursors of the literature produced in this period and beyond. More than this, the Writings provide both the warrant for such literature and some of the interpretative paradigms that will be used to relate scripture and community in these new times of persecution and change.

At this point we must return briefly to the question of canon and the Writings. Scholarly opinion is divided on whether the Writings at this time are a part of a closed Hebrew canon, or whether during this period the canon is still open to further "writings." The value of the Writings as interpretive norms for Jewish and Christian communities is not dependent upon deciding whether or not there is a closed canon. Surely, many of the Writings must have been authoritative, even attaining scriptural status, in this period. However, this does not necessarily point to a closed canon. The thesis of this study is that a closed canon in an early period (200 B.C.E. to the turn of the eras) does not explain adequately the nature and intention of the intertestamental literature or the New Testament. The Writings themselves testify to Torah and Prophets as scripture. The literature subsequent to the Writings is best viewed as further writings, intended to be used authoritatively as responses to Torah and Prophets. Only at a later date do Jewish and Christian communities consider their canons closed. In this period, there are many "writings," some more authoritative than others, some to become a part of canon, some not.

It seems to follow, therefore, both that the early pseudepigrapha were composed during a period in which the limits of the canon apparently remained fluid at least to some Jews, and that some Jews and Christians inherited and passed on these documents as inspired. They did not necessarily regard them as apocryphal, or outside a canon. . . . This brief overview of the historical development of the canons reveals that to call the Pseudepigrapha "non-canonical," or the biblical books "canonical," can be historically inaccurate prior to A.D. 100 and the period in which most of these documents were written. These terms should be used as an expression of some later "orthodoxy" with regard to a collection that is well defined regarding what belongs within and what is to be excluded from it. It is potentially misleading to use the terms "non-canonical," "canonical," "heresy," and "orthodoxy" when describing either Early Judaism or Early Christianity."[8]

The Writings provide an important perspective from which we may view the developments found in intertestamental literature, the New Testament, and rabbinic literature. The interrelationship between text and community that produced the responses of the Writings continued. Although the Writings reflect a stabilization of Torah and Prophets, the diversity of the responses found in the Writings provides both the explanation and the rationale for further developments. As the Writings represent a response to new events and concerns in the community of faith by the light of an emerging scripture, so also does the literature that follows.

The Writings also provide one means of categorizing subsequent literature. This does not appear to be merely coincidental. Rather, the types of responses reflected in the Writings represent basic needs and basic interpretive paradigms that many, if not all, scriptural communities will utilize. The questions of what to do with Torah and Prophets and how they are to be used in discerning the will of God in new situations remain fundamental for all subsequent communities. Moreover, the answers given by the Writings need to be considered seriously by all. Although many of the uses made of scripture from 200 B.C.E. to 200 C.E. will be judged nonauthoritative by later generations of Christians and Jews, the process begun in the Writings and continued into this later period will ultimately result in the completed canons of both Christians (Old Testament–New Testament) and Jews (Tanak-Talmud).[9] The Writings represent a critical point in the development of the content, scope, and form of canon in Jewish and Christian communities.

The remainder of this chapter will focus on intertestamental, the New Testament, and early rabbinic literature. Our primary focus will be the value of using the interpretive paradigms found in the Writings for understanding the nature and shape of these further "writings." Although many new events played a crucial role in shaping the form and message of this new literature, there is also continuity between these later writers and their communities and those of the Writings. Also, we will reexamine the issue of the development of the canon in light of the preceding discussions. Our primary concern will be to assess the function and value of using the concept of canon when discussing the literary developments of this period.

INTERTESTAMENTAL LITERATURE

The literature to be surveyed in this section is found in three primary textual corpora: the Apocrypha, Qumran manuscripts, and the Pseudcpigrapha. The bulk of this literature is provisionally dated between 200 B.C.E. and 200 C.E. Determining the provenance for much of it is difficult. Most of it was composed in either Judea or Egypt. Other texts could be studied with benefit (e.g., Philo, Josephus), but the literature surveyed here should provide a representative picture of the responses to scripture in this period and the way in which the Writings may illuminate them. A primary criterion for choosing this literature has been its relationship to and explicit use of scripture. There is no attempt to provide a chronological development of intertestamental literature here. Rather, the types of literature produced, at whatever times, will be related to the types of literature found in the Writings to ascertain if the Writings can be used to explain and conceptualize the purposes of these other "writings."

After the early post-exilic period (538 B.C.E. to roughly 200 B.C.E.), in which time our primary literary sources are the Writings, the later post-exilic period virtually explodes with a "voluminous and varied literature."[10] Whatever the reasons for the comparative lack of written material in earlier times, the new conditions of persecution, the changes in the Near Eastern world power structure (from Ptolemaic or Seleucid to Roman), and the challenges to Jewish identity and existence in this period create the occasion for much literary production in all places where Jewish communities are found.

Several primary concerns characterize this literature in varying degrees. First, the centrality of Torah is very often a focal point. Much of this literature, whatever its form or ultimate message, maintains that a strict adherence or obedience to the Law (Torah) is necessary. Torah often provides the figures to which pseudonymous works are attributed

(Moses, Joseph, Abraham, and so forth). Often, the texts of Torah are explicated, expanded, or supplemented through various methods. Despite the diversity found in this literature, the centrality of Torah remains.

Second, the Prophets are also of great importance to the intertestamental writers. The oppression and upheaval of the period caused many communities to use the prophetic literature in an eschatological manner and to look forward to a time when the Messiah would return and when the new age would be ushered in. On the one hand, much of the literature that utilizes prophetic texts and concerns is apocalyptic in nature. In view of persecution and the need to identify and sometimes separate Jewish communities from others, this is not surprising. On the other hand, there are many uses of the Prophets that, although stressing the eschatological, do not use apocalyptic forms and imagery (e.g., angelology, visions, heavenly journeys). There is ultimately no clear division between texts that focus on Torah and those that focus on Prophets, thus reflecting the need to relate to both of these scriptural bodies. For example, the centrality of Torah is often witnessed to in the apocalyptic literature through the use of Torah figures (e.g., Enoch) and in the Deuteronomic literature through the use of retributional systems.

A third concern to which much of this literature responds is the relationship of the faith community to culture, to the world in which it finds itself. Some communities reject the influences of the outside world (e.g., Qumran), whereas others employ Greek thought and rhetoric to express their message (e.g., Wisdom of Solomon). To accommodate or not remains a vital concern in the literature of this period, with many proponents on each side of the issue.

Fourth, a concern closely related to the issue of accommodation is best described as ethical. Despite the sometimes esoteric character of much of this literature, it wrestles frequently with questions of right or wrong, and with the appropriate action to be taken in light of difficult circumstances. Whether this is determined by a complicated trip to the heavens through visionary imagery or through an exegesis of a Torah precept, the question of how to live life righteously and well is important.

A fifth concern of the intertestamental literature focuses on worship and piety. In addition to liturgical literature produced at this time, prayers, descriptions of fasting, and adherence to the Law are also found within many nonliturgical texts. Although visions differ and interpretations of Torah and Prophets diverge, all are reminded of the centrality of worship and of a piety rooted in prayer and a receptivity to God's continuing revelation and direction for the individual and the community.

The methods used to present these concerns differ dramatically. The use of midrash, legends, visions, prayers, magic, and mystical journeys are only a few of the various devices by which these authors present their messages. For most of these communities, the crises that prompted and produced this literature were theological in nature. It would be difficult if not impossible to forget that God's will and purpose for Israel was the central issue. That this will and purpose had to be related to scripture, despite the mixture of priorities, of methods, of purposes, and of social settings, is also a major testimony of all of the literature before us.

If the concerns that the intertestamental literature address are many, so are the literary forms used to express these concerns. A brief overview of the categories used to distinguish and define the pseudepigraphal literature in the recent work edited by Professor James Charlesworth provides an entry into this area.[11] Many of these writings are characterized as apocalyptic literature. Although much of this literature contains elements (e.g., heavenly journey) not found in Daniel, overall the basic characteristics of the form remain the same. The "testament" literature is more difficult to define in terms of its form. There is usually a scenario portraying an ideal figure (e.g., a patriarch) facing death and giving a final exhortation to those who remain behind. However, the contents of the testaments may include apocalyptic visions, wisdom teaching, ethical injunctions, and midrashic exegesis.

A second category, the "expansions" of the Old Testament and legends, seeks to clarify, expand, and explicate stories found in Torah in the light of new needs and concerns of the contemporary faith community. God's guidance in history, the importance of covenant, and other central concerns of scripture are highlighted in order to exhort the present community to faithful action. The special election and status of Judaism are often stressed, although appearances to the contrary sometimes cause eschatological motifs to appear.

Wisdom and philosophical literature in this period, a third category, is similar to that found in the Writings with two important qualifications. Most of this literature is not associated with Solomon. The increasing importance of contemporary sages may help to explain this fact. Also, although scholars have often posited that Ecclesiastes reflects the influence of Greek philosophy, most of the Writings are free from such influence. In the intertestamental literature, however, there is much use of Greek philosophical rhetoric, literary forms, and terminology.[12] Surely, the use of these forms to speak of Torah and Prophets was helpful to some and offensive to others.

Prayers, psalms, and odes, a fourth category, are very similar to the literature found in Psalms and Lamentations. Whether such material, especially the psalms found at Qumran, is indicative of an open canon for the Psalter is a matter of much debate. Indeed, fragments from many diverse works represent concerns of chronography, philosophy, oracular material, drama, history, poetry, romance, and mysticism. Although these fragments themselves need to be related to more completely preserved works, they do widen our knowledge and appreciation of the many forms and functions intertestamental literature used.[13]

It is important to note that the categories used to describe the literature of the Pseudepigrapha by Charlesworth and others are imprecise in many cases. Such an observation should not be seen as a critique of modern scholarship but rather reflective of the literature itself. For example, very often apocalyptic material contains prayers and other types of literature, testaments may include almost anything, and the "expansions" take many different forms. The mixture of forms that characterizes much of intertestamental literature represents the wide interests, purposes, and backgrounds of its authors as well as the audiences to which they are addressed.

When Charlesworth's categories are applied to the literature of the Apocrypha and Qumran, most of this latter literature fits easily into one classification or another. However, at Qumran, the Community Rule and the commentaries (*pesherim*) on individual prophetic books represent new genres. The former has no real parallels with contemporary Jewish literature, although comparisons with the later Apostolic Constitutions and the Didache are often made. The *pesher* literature and the midrashic fragments have parallels with later rabbinic literature. In the Apocrypha, the historical material of 1–2 Maccabees is probably closer in form to Ezra–Nehemiah and 1–2 Chronicles than to the material with historical interest in the other intertestamental literature. Yet, this is a matter of degree, not kind.

This brief overview of the types of literature found in this period reflects continuity and discontinuity with the Writings. In order to discern how important the Writings are in providing precedent and paradigmatic control for this subsequent literature, it is necessary to examine the Apocrypha, the Qumran literature, and the Pseudepigrapha to determine how the five basic literary and hermeneutical divisions of the Writings have influenced them.

We have seen that the Writings, in their diversity of form and content, represent five basic ways to respond to Torah and Prophets—five ways to interpret and present their messages to a scriptural community. First, the Writings include *sapiential literature*, which, often proverbial in form, has wisdom as a central purpose or goal (Job, Proverbs, Ecclesiastes, Song of Songs). Second, the Writings include *liturgical literature*, which is to be used individually or corporately (Psalms, Lamentations). Third, the Writings include *historical literature*, which seeks as its central purpose to present the history of Israel and Judah in light of contemporary concerns (Ezra, Nehemiah, 1–2 Chronicles). Fourth, the Writings include *apocalyptic literature*, which intends to provide direction and hope for the oppressed and righteous community (Daniel). Fifth, the Writings include *edifying literature*, which presents paradigms for behavior through story forms and, sometimes, a morale boost for the people (Ruth, Esther, [Daniel 1–6?]).

The literature of the Apocrypha presents all five types of literature found in the Writings. The Wisdom of Solomon and Ecclesiasticus stand firmly within the category of sapiential literature. Ecclesiasticus reflects the development of Torah centrality through its equation of wisdom with Torah (24:23ff.). Although some have argued that the concept of an eternal Torah is influenced by Hellenistic thought, others have seen this as a continuation of the long-held notion that wisdom is to be associated with the creative activity of God. "For Sirach it is the perception of Torah as the wisdom of God, not the eternality of Torah, which is the chief issue at stake."[14] Nevertheless, the Wisdom of Solomon, with its use of Greek philosophical terminology and its eschatological perspective, represents a combination of Hebrew wisdom, prophetic and Torah traditions, with Greek thought that provides a message to Jews in the Diaspora (Egypt).

Liturgical literature is represented by the Book of Baruch and the Prayer of Manasseh. In Baruch the law is the sum of all wisdom, and the instruction to read the book with its penitential prayer and hymn at public occasions justifies its placement in liturgical literature, although close associations with wisdom and edifying literature should be noted. The Prayer of Manasseh is clearly a liturgical piece, demonstrating the increasing emphasis on penitence and confession in the post-exilic period. The prayer is more closely associated with, and probably influenced by, the picture of Manasseh found in 2 Chronicles than that in 2 Kings. Thus, this is liturgical literature responding directly to the Writings and the developments represented there.

Historical literature in the Apocrypha is represented by 1–2 Maccabees and 1 Esdras. The centrality of Torah and the presence of special sources (letters) in 1–2 Maccabees recall some of the characteristics of Ezra–Nehemiah. First Esdras is, in part, an independent translation of material in 2 Chronicles, Ezra, and Nehemiah. All of this historical literature contains material illustrating later developments in Jewish thought: the growing importance of wisdom (2 Esdras), creation "ex nihilo," and resurrection motifs (2 Maccabees).

The Apocrypha also contains much edifying literature. The additions to Esther and Daniel 1–6 in the Septuagint function to intensify the heroic and pietistic qualities of central figures in these books. The books of Judith and Tobit are also edifying literature and stress obedience to the law through a variety of means (prayer, fasting, wisdom). Finally, the Letter of Jeremiah, clearly relying on the authoritative picture of this prophet in the scriptural corpus, warns against assimilation and idolatry.

It is interesting to note that there is only one example of apocalyptic literature in the Apocrypha—2 Esdras. This apocalypse reflects evidence of later Christian editing, demonstrating the importance and use of this type of literature for both Christians and Jews of this period. Because this literature is widespread at Qumran and in the Pseudepigrapha, its relative paucity in the Apocrypha may be significant. Two possible reasons for this are the time and place of composition of most of the Apocrypha and the issue of canon. Because much of the Apocrypha dates from early in the period we are surveying, it may be that the communities involved did not feel such cataclysmic literature was yet appropriate. Or, the Egyptian community that collected this literature may have intentionally rejected this type of literature. The issue of canon and Apocrypha raised by this suggestion will be discussed below.

The sectarian community at Qumran produced literature that can, generally, fit within the categories the Writings represent. The commentary on Psalm 37 is a clear example of sapiential literature applying a retributional theology of the wisdom psalm to the contemporary conflicts and struggles of this community. The Hymn scroll and various liturgical fragments demonstrate the importance of composing new liturgical literature, with the Psalms as an obvious model. There is no good example of historical literature at Qumran, although the Damascus Rule may serve to demonstrate the importance of this type of writing. The Genesis Apocryphon, the Words of Moses, and the Prayer of Nabonidus correspond to the category of edifying literature. The importance of the Law, the expansions or explications of Torah material, and of Daniel (Nabonidus) show the central role of scripture in this community's life. Finally, eschatological and, more specifically, apocalyptic literature is represented by the commentaries on Isaiah, Micah, Nahum, Hosea, and Habakkuk, as well as the War Rule and Messianic Rule. Concerns with end times, the coming of the Messiah, and the fulfillment of prophecy all demonstrate the importance of the Prophets for this community.

In addition to the new literature written, the Qumran community also produced many manuscripts of biblical material. In view of the community's conviction that the end time was imminent and their strict adherence to a particular interpretation of Torah and Prophets, there may have been no desire or need to write historical commentaries. In one sense their time was frozen; they were waiting for an end to their community that would, and did, come soon. Issues of continuity and the future were dealt with by the Community Rule, but even this was seen as temporary. The relatively small amount of wisdom literature produced may reflect the rejection of the scribally dominated traditions of Jerusalem. The central role of the priests (versus the sages) at Qumran may be further evidence of this rejection.

When the vast literature of the Pseudepigrapha is surveyed, examples of all types of literature found in the Writings are represented. Further, with the exceptions noted above, the typology we have found in the Writings seems adequate to organize this literature. The sapiential literature found in the Pseudepigrapha is relatively sparse in comparison to most other types. Pseudo-Phocyclides, the Sentences of Meander, the Testament of Job, and perhaps the Testament of the Three Patriarchs are the best examples, although interspersed with other (historical, edifying) concerns as well. One explanation for the relatively small amount of sapiential literature follows directly from our observations about the scribal tradition above. If the sages and scribes are the guardians and primary transmitters of the scriptures, their task would be to interpret and conserve what already exists rather than to produce new literature. Some have suggested, in light of later Talmudic traditions, that there was an interdict against further writing by the sages in this period.[15] Because the evidence for such an interdict is not contemporary with this period, it seems wiser to assume that the sages and scribes had all they could handle in interpreting and conserving the scriptures and, perhaps, that sapiential literature was not the pressing need of the day. Because virtually all other types of literature produced in this period reflect the influence of sapiential thought, we need not, however, assume that sages were uninvolved in their composition. Moreover, other developments in rabbinic literature and the central role of the sages there need to be examined when speaking of this important body of teachers and critics.[16]

Liturgical literature is amply represented by the Psalms of Solomon, the Prayer of Joseph, and various synagogal prayers. Again, the Psalms provide a model. The incorporation of contemporary political and theological concerns is noteworthy. Although the liturgical literature of this period is not insignificant, in comparison with historical, edifying, and apocalyptic literature it represents a relatively small corpus. This may point either to the sufficiency of already existent liturgical literature (e.g., the Psalms) or to the needs of the day, which called for different types of messages.

There is a great deal of historical literature in the Pseudepigrapha. Fourth Baruch, 3 Maccabees, the Letter of Aristeas, Jubilees, the Lives of the Prophets, and the Ladder of Jacob reflect concerns either to comment upon past history as found in Torah and Prophets in view of the new needs of the day or to speak of contemporary history in light of past authoritative teachings. Although we do not find equivalents of Ezra–Nehemiah or the Chronicles here, the importance of interpreting the present in light of past historical narratives is illustrated. The Testaments of Moses, Solomon, and Adam may also be added to this historical literature, even though their primary concern seems not to highlight the authoritative value of the past as much as to edify.

Edifying literature in the Pseudepigrapha is plentiful. In addition to the testaments mentioned above, Jannes and Jambres, the History of Joseph, 4 Maccabees, the Testament of the Twelve, Joseph and Asenath, and the Lives of Adam and Eve fit into this category. In addition to the use of traditions and texts found in Torah and Prophets, this literature incorporates magical concerns (Jannes and Jambres), folktales, and other nonscriptural elements. Common to much of this edifying literature are the centrality of Torah and obedience to it as essential for righteousness and deliverance.

By far the most common type of pseudepigraphal literature produced in this period is apocalyptic in nature. In view of the historical conditions, this is hardly surprising. The History of the Rechabites, 1–3 Enoch, the Sibylline Oracles, the Treatise of Shem, 4 Ezra, and the Apocalypses of Zephaniah, Abraham, and Adam are representative of but do not exhaust this literature. Angelology, heavenly journeys, visions of the end, dualism, messianism—all utilizing texts from Torah,

Prophets, and the Writings (particularly Daniel)—are found here. It is difficult to explain all of this literature, some of it dependent upon non-Hebrew oracular sources (the Sibyl), solely in terms of the sociological situation of persecution. If we do so, we must suggest that the majority of the minority was persecuted! Indeed, in light of what we know of Judaism and Christianity in this period, this may well be the case. However, the prevalence of this literature suggests that apocalyptic or at least eschatological concerns and rhetoric were fairly common in this period. Such an observation leads us to affirm the importance of the Prophets in explaining and interpreting the events of the day.[17] There was a consensus about obedience to the Torah attested by all the intertestamental literature. There was also a drive to interpret that obedience and Torah in the light of God's promises for restoration found in the Prophets. Such a need may not have been universal, but it was more than simply the response of a few. Torah, Prophets, and the tension between them characterized by the responses of the Writings were continued into this period by the intertestamental literature.

Four concluding questions and observations are in order. First, it is clear that the period from 200 B.C.E. produced a great amount of literature that does not fit easily into any of the interpretive paradigms of the Writings. However, when scripture is of central import to the authors of intertestamental literature, many similarities can be found. At the most general level, this literature continues the interaction between a community of the book and the needs facing that community. For the Writings, the "book" of these communities appears to be Torah and Prophets, although some of the Writings are also important. A study of the provenance of this literature suggests that this activity was occurring wherever Jewish communities lived.

Second, our categorization of the intertestamental literature necessarily relied upon generalizations of complex and multifaceted books. Yet, it appears that this literature may be seen as a continuation of the sapiential, liturgical, historical, edifying, and apocalyptic interpretive patterns found in the Writings. Surely many new elements are added, but such an observation is detrimental to a thesis of continuity only if we assume that the Writings are to be viewed as authoritative and normative in content. If, as we suggest, however, the Writings are normative primarily (if at all) in terms of the interpretive paradigms they exemplify and in terms of the mandated process of interaction between text and community they reflect, then the addition of "new" content and "new" methods is not only understandable but also to be expected.

Third, the intertestamental period witnesses to a continuation of a literary production in part explained by the pluralism of scripture, more specifically the Torah and Prophets. Continuity with the interpretive and literary patterns found within the Writings merely affirms our assessment of that earlier literary response to scriptural pluralism. Whether we may speak of a general pattern of religion that characterized all Judaism of this period is difficult to determine.[18] On the one hand, the centrality of Torah and Prophets is clear. On the other hand, the diversity of responses and the fact that these responses were not necessarily to be related to all communities and their missions make such a thesis difficult. Still, the mixture of Torah, Prophets, and the various interpretive paradigms found in the Writings in this subsequent literature suggests a picture of communities that have much in common. To be sure, there were Hellenists, sectarian responses such as the Qumran community, Pharisees, Sadducees, and messianic visionaries. Nevertheless, the centrality of scripture for all of these and others suggests that a common matrix necessary for a genuine pluralism—rather than a series of diverse and essentially unrelated communities—is in place.

Finally, we conclude our study of the intertestamental literature by affirming that the Writings provide an adequate lens through which to view and categorize the literature that followed it and also that in a very real sense this subsequent literature represents a continuation of the Writings. In view of the vast amount of literature produced in this period, we can foresee some potential problems. The continuation of the Writings is perhaps too inclusive, too successful. The consensus about Torah, Prophets, and some of the Writings is being strained by the diversity and voluminous amount of interpretation occurring. Or is it? Must scripture be seen to be a manageable and easily comprehended body of literature? Is not the question a different one? Must scripture, whatever its contents, at least be the common property of all? Torah and Prophets are surely common property. The Writings appear to be common to many, but the literature that continues what the Writings have begun is not. The resolution of what is or is not scripture is becoming an issue. It will be resolved not merely or even primarily by the decisions of an intellectual or hierarchical elite, but rather by new revelations of God in community, to which these decisions will be, as with the Writings, a response.

THE NEW TESTAMENT WRITINGS

The primary purpose of this section is to assess the value of the Writings for understanding the nature and shape of the literature that ultimately becomes the New Testament. Although it is not presupposed that this post-exilic literature can fully explain how the New Testament material arose or the forms in which its messages occur, it is suggested that the Writings provide an important backdrop for understanding the process and some of the ordering that is represented there.

Several questions arise in light of our study to this point. Are the Writings functioning in a paradigmatic manner for the authors of the New Testament literature? Are these books and letters to be seen, like the intertestamental literature, as further "writings"? Conversely, do the *New* Testament books represent something very *new*, which makes continuity difficult to assume or propose? Or is the New Testament a little bit of new and old, with the result being a new combination of the interpretive traditions of the past and revelatory events of the present?

One special problem, not shared with intertestamental literature, deserves mention at this point. By the end of our period, 200 C.E., the New Testament writings were functioning as a collection and not simply as disparate voices in many different communities. Brevard Childs has aptly described this phenomenon.

> With the growth of a written corpus of acknowledged authoritative writings which reached its first stage of stabilization by the end of the second century, a new literary dynamic was set in motion. The written word not only became the vehicle of the gospel tradition, but provided an interpretation of tradition which often transcended the earlier stages of its growth. . . . The written word thus assumed an autonomy which it had not first possessed, but one which continued to show continuity with its origins by firmly attaching its authority to Jesus Christ, the sole source of the Good News.[19]

This development has parallels with the formation of Torah and Prophets in the early post-exilic period. The implications of a *collection* of writings are significant. In addition to evaluating the Writings and the New Testament from the perspective of the types of literary responses made by each corpus, attention can and should also be given to larger literary structures within the New Testament in an effort to determine what influence the Torah, Prophets, and Writings had in generating and shaping the literature of the early Christians.

One significant phenomenon that explicitly reflects the importance of Jewish scripture for the New Testament writers is the presence of scriptural quotations in this new literature. With the exception of the Song of Solomon, scholars have found direct quotations or allusions to material contained in all books of the Hebrew Bible. The vast majority of the passages used are from Torah and Prophets. There is one important exception within the Writings, the Psalms. This book takes on special importance for two reasons. First, with Isaiah, the most often quoted book in the New Testament is the Psalms. Second, Psalms is quoted prophetically; that is, the messianic nature of this book is stressed, with David becoming a prophet of the highest order whose words, in the Psalms, predict the coming of Jesus the Christ. Clearly Psalms was well known, probably because of its central place in the worship life of the people. The prophetic reading of this literature had already begun in the post-exilic period (e.g., 1–2 Chronicles).

In addition to references to particular books, specific figures, and verses, the New Testament writers also use more general terminology to refer both to larger parts of scripture and to the entire scriptural corpus. Thus, the "law" is often used to refer to Torah and the "prophets" to the canonical division of the same name. However, the Writings are not referred to explicitly, suggesting at the very least that this term was probably not in use at this time. Nevertheless, there is evidence that a three-part canon was recognized through the use of phrases like "the law of Moses and the prophets and the Psalms" (Luke 24:44). The New Testament writers also use words such as *graphe, grapho*, and *anaginosko* to refer to all the written, or read, scriptures. On the one hand, the evidence from the New Testament quotations and allusions to scripture suggests that virtually all of the Hebrew literature, including the Writings, was authoritative in this period. On the other hand, the extent to which the Writings, as a canonical division, are both fully defined and a closed, stable collection, is not clear.[20] The fact that some of the quotations of Torah, Prophets, and Writings in the New Testament are clearly from the text of the Septuagint rather than from the Hebrew text further heightens our uncertainty. Moreover, the inclusion of quotations from both the apocryphal literature (e.g., Ecclesiasticus and the Wisdom of Solomon) and pseudepigraphal material suggests the possibility of a fluid and open, not yet fully defined or closed, canon for the New Testament writers.

The use of quotations and traditions found in scripture demonstrates continuity with the intertestamental literature. Virtually all of the present Hebrew Bible was used and seen as authoritative, although there is evidence that the scriptures were a larger and not yet fully defined body of literature. The dialogue between community and text mirrored in the Writings is continued, but the Writings themselves are now seen as authoritative as well.

The New Testament writers share the historical context in which much of the intertestamental literature was composed and circulated. Indeed, some of the later pseudepigraphal literature reflects a Christian editing for particular church communities. Although attention to other early Christian writings lies beyond the scope of our study, it must be remembered that a great deal of literature explicitly Christian in origin was composed in this period did not, finally, become part of the canon. As with the Old Testament Pseudepigrapha, we should assume such writings had authority for particular communities, much like the writings that ultimately became the New Testament.[21]

In addition to sharing the historical context and being exposed to much of the intertestamental literature, the early Jewish-Christian writers also shared the process that produced both the Writings and the other literature we have studied; that is to say, the New Testament literature reflects an interrelationship between authoritative scripture (Torah, Prophets, and most of the Writings) and the needs, questions, concerns, and new events of the Christian communities. Thus, the diversity of the New Testament and other early Christian writings may be seen as a continuation of the same diversity found in other contemporary literature in light of the different needs, experiences, and backgrounds of the communities of faith. At the same time, there is also a consensus reflected in this literature that scripture was of central importance and that it constituted a necessary component in understanding, explaining, and living in the world. Childs, utilizing Campenhausen, has summarized this consensus of the earliest Christians in the following manner: "In light of the Old Testament which was acknowledged to be the true oracles of God, how was one to understand the Good News of Jesus Christ?"[22]

Having discussed some of the elements that the authors of the Writings, the intertestamental literature, and the New Testament held in common, it is essential to remember what they did not share, namely, the experience of Jesus Christ viewed in a particular way. All biblical literature is testimony to different needs and different views of God's will and purpose. Further, we are also often able to identify common needs (worship, instruction, community building, etc.). Moreover, the New Testament writers, despite their diversity, all profess Jesus to be the Messiah, all profess him to be the "good news." This profession is rooted in a new experience and one not common to all. The effects of this new revelation of God for the early church are far-reaching in terms of the literature produced, the interpretive paradigms used, the norms developed, and the subsequent growth of the church. Although we believe the Writings can be valuable in understanding the responses made to Jesus by the early church, the newness of the early Christian experience and its normative value cannot be downplayed.

If we compare the types of literature found in the Writings to the New Testament literature as we did for the intertestamental literature, some of the implications of the newness of the Christian experience become manifest. On the one hand, we do find some clear parallels. The Book of Revelation is definitely apocalyptic literature. Moreover, the influence of this type of literature and thought pervades much of the New Testament.[23] The Book of Acts would seem to be a type of historical literature. Further, although the epistolary literature represents a different genre, its purposes to edify, teach, admonish, and exhort are not incompatible with purposes in the sapiential and edifying literature of the Writings. On the other hand, the genre of "gospel" does not seem to correspond closely to any of the Writings material, although the collection of stories and other types of material around a central authoritative figure is not a new phenomenon. Here the normative nature of the revelation in Jesus Christ changes some of the interpretive dynamics we have found in earlier responses to scripture. In sum, we do not find that the Writings can be categorized in such a way as to provide clear analogues for most of the New Testament literature. Still, many of the needs represented by the communities of the Writings—to build community, to worship, to instruct, to edify— are clearly reflected both in the literature of the New Testament and in the dialogue with scripture that is a necessary prerequisite for meeting these needs and ascertaining the will of God.

If the Writings as types of literary responses to Torah and Prophets are not as helpful in explaining the New Testament as they are for intertestamental literature, they do have value in helping us to understand the way in which this literature was collected and ordered. The different literary sources and communal experiences of the early church gradually merge into collections, and these collections have important parallels with the Hebrew Bible.

We begin with a structural comparison that takes seriously the tripartite division of the Hebrew Bible and attempts to find analogues with the New Testament.

In such a comparison the only real literary parallel between the Writings and the New Testament is found in Revelation. However, one difficulty with such a parallel is the epistolary form of Revelation and its claim to be prophetic.

Hebrew Bible	*New Testament*
Torah	Gospels
Prophets	Epistles
1. Former Prophets	1. Acts
2. Latter Prophets	2. Paul and others
Writings	Revelation

A more accurate comparison might look like this:

Hebrew Bible	*New Testament*
Torah	Gospels
Prophets	Epistles
1. Former Prophets	1. Acts
2. Latter Prophets	2. Paul and others
Writings	

Such a comparison has much to commend it. We acknowledge both that such parallels have a synthetic and artificial flavor *and* that their value goes beyond the bounds of positing some historical intention on the part of the early church to create collections on the basis of such perceived parallelism. Nevertheless, there is evidence in the early church that the Gospels were seen to be the new Torah and the writings of at least Paul to be analogous to the Prophets. This is true not only for the truncated version of the New Testament used by Marcion (Gospel and Apostle), but more significantly for Clement of Alexandria (Law and Prophets = the Gospel with the Apostles).[24]

Perhaps the most significant and initially distressing observation to be made is the virtual absence of the Writings in the New Testament. They simply have no analogues in this second structural comparison; there are no "writings" in the New Testament, were such a parallelism to be used. If such be the case, what is the value of the Writings for understanding the nature and composition of the New Testament? Perhaps the best way to describe their value is by making one more schematic comparison. Here the Writings stand midway between the authoritative scripture of Torah-Prophets and Gospels-Epistles. This is an accurate historical picture. The Writings function not primarily to provide normative interpretive paradigms of response, although we have seen that sometimes this has occurred.

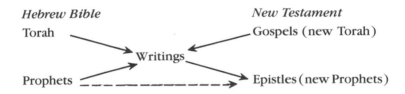

Rather—and this has been confirmed many times—the Writings point toward Torah and Prophets, suggesting new and old ways to appropriate the messages of this scripture in light of new problems and new revelations. In one sense the Writings are invisible in the New Testament. Yet, without the paradigmatic precedent and function of the Writings that point us, in a variety of ways, to Torah and Prophets, it is difficult to explain the *new* Torah and *new* Prophets of the early church.

Despite the fact that the Writings are not very visible, the New Testament is a continuation of the process of response to Torah and Prophets begun there. In this sense, at least, the New Testament literature is simply more "writings," on the one hand. On the other hand, the new revelations of God to the early church have created norms and interpretive shifts that will ultimately cause a new scripture to be formed, with new priorities and new ways of reading and living God's story. This is always at issue in a scriptural community—the mixture of old and new is always an uncertain element. This surely occurred at Qumran and in several other communities that produced intertestamental literature in light of new revelations. The New Testament reflects the consensus about the centrality of scripture, however interpreted, which the Writings represent. The New Testament also reflects the diversity that the Writings represent, even warrant. Something new has happened, with definitive consequences for the old and for the shape of scripture itself. However, even this, the mixture of new and old, is "old" to the Writings, to which the New Testament writers are surely heirs.

RABBINIC LITERATURE

Although most rabbinic literature produced by Jewish sages (rabbis) is dated after 200 C.E., it is important for the purposes of this study to discuss briefly its characteristics and level of continuity with the Writings. A portion of this literature, at least the Babylonian and Jerusalem Talmuds, came to have a canonical status similar to the New

Testament. That is, Judaism has, like Christianity, a two-part canon.[25] The role of the Writings in this canon is discussed below. The fact that the formative traditions of this material are often located in the period we are now assessing makes mention of it both appropriate and incumbent.

Unlike most of the intertestamental literature and the New Testament, the early rabbinic literature is difficult to date with precision. Part of this is due to the nature of our sources, which in their present form reflect a compilation and transmission process that occurred several centuries later.

Even when the early rabbis are quoted, we cannot always be sure these statements accurately reflect the times to which they refer. In addition, there is a curious lack of rabbinic teaching from about 200 B.C.E. to the middle of the first century C.E., which has sometimes been explained as the result of a ban or interdict upon the writing down of oral teaching. In any case, an evaluation of the nature and scope of rabbinic activity and thought before at least the first century C.E. is difficult.

Before we compare the Writings with subsequent rabbinic literature, an overview of the types of literature produced by the rabbis and some general comments about its nature and intention are in order. There is no attempt here to be comprehensive. We wish rather to provide a sketch that gives a taste of this rich literature. Some of the standard terminology applied to rabbinic teaching is anachronistic for this period, but in order to provide a meaningful discussion we will use it anyway.

Samuel Sandmel's summarization of the rabbinic literature can begin our discussion.

> This huge body of writings might be divided into three categories: one, the Midrashim; two, Mishna and Gemara; and three, the Targumim. The Midrashim are commentaries on Scripture arranged according to the sequence of the biblical verses. The Mishna is a laconic statement of the secondary laws (*halacha*) derived from Scripture. The Targumim allude to the Aramaic translation of Scripture; these translations have come down to us in differing styles and in somewhat differing ages.[26]

For our purposes the literature that interprets scripture, namely, the Talmuds (Mishnah and Gemarah) of Babylon and Jerusalem and the Midrashim are most important.

Two comprehensive terms are often used to categorize the types of literature found in rabbinic literature: halachah and haggadah. Halachic interpretation is composed of the teachings, rules, or statutes of the sages. Its concern is with the following of the Law, although in pursuing this interest any scriptural passage, Torah or not, may be interpreted. Haggadah consists of all scriptural interpretation that is nonhalachic in character. Although there is more halachah than haggadah in rabbinic literature, E. P. Sanders has noted the importance of the latter for our understanding of rabbinic Judaism.

> Any construction of the principles of Rabbinic religion . . . must ultimately rely a great deal on haggadah—that large body of material which covers everything which the Rabbis did not consider law. It is in haggadah that one finds whatever statements there are about the significance of Torah, the understanding of the covenant, what one must do to be saved and the like. And it is haggadah that many Rabbinic scholars have singled out as especially revealing a general consensus.[27]

Generally speaking, the Midrashim are haggadic and the Mishnah-Gemarah is halachic. However, Mishnah has haggadic material and the Midrashim have halachic material. Further, there is haggadic interpretation of Torah as well as halachic interpretation of Prophets and Writings. Although the content and intention of rabbinic teachings must be analyzed individually to determine their nature and intention, these larger terms are helpful in defining both the purpose of scriptural interpretation and, often, the kind of interpretation that will be found in a particular written corpus.

Although the Midrashim date from periods later than the intertestamental literature and the New Testament, they reflect a process of interpretation that has its roots much earlier.

> The constantly changing conditions of life required new regulations . . . as far back as the times of Ezra or the period immediately succeeding, the law was maintained or enlarged by the scholars in a manner suitable to the post-exilic conditions through the operation of scriptural exposition, *midrash*. . . . The grounding of a statute in Scripture by means of subtle interpretation served, in the first place, to widen the written Law so as to meet new conditions. Secondly, it imparted to the oral law the requisite authority.[28]

We have already seen in the Writings themselves that the books of 1–2 Chronicles and Daniel (9:24–27) have been characterized as a type of *midrash.* Various methods are used in midrash, but the basic component appears to be the discussion of particular scriptural verses for purposes of application to contemporary problems and needs. Sometimes the purpose of midrash is less clear, however.

> For in midrash the Bible becomes ... a world unto itself. Midrashic exegesis is the way into that world; it does not seek to view present-day reality through biblical spectacles, neither to find referents of biblical prophecy in present-day happenings, nor referents to the daily life of the soul in biblical allegory. Instead it simply overwhelms the present; the Bible's time is important, while the present is not; and so it invites the reader to cross over into the enterable world of Scripture.[29]

Lest midrash be viewed as escapism, we must reassert our premise that the interpretation of scripture found in the Writings and rabbinic literature arises from contemporary needs, however difficult it may be to determine what these needs are or how they are met by certain types of interpretation. Midrashic exegesis is sometimes easily and intentionally applicable to contemporary problems; at other times we cannot fathom its mysteries without entering its particular world.

The most important literary corpus of scriptural interpretation—or at least the one that has become normative for Judaism—is the Talmud—in Babylonian and Jerusalem forms and provenances. This vast literature contains first the teachings of the early sages (*Tannaim*) up to the time of the collection made by Rabbi Juda ha-Nasi in the second century C.E. This collection is called the Mishnah. The second constitutive part of the Talmud consists of the discussions of the Mishnah by the second great division of sages, the Amoraim, and is called Gemarah. The Talmud is a complex literary corpus divided into long tractates covering different topics. It is difficult for the uninitiated to read, as it resembles more the minutes of a constitutional convention than, for example, a biblical commentary.

All of the rabbinic material reveals the centrality of the Law and the need to obey it. The ways in which scripture is explicated are diverse and often confusing to those not familiar with it. The mixture of halachic and haggadic literature produced by the sages in this period reflects diverse needs of the community and many uses of scripture. It also points to the central importance of the sage for formulation of this interpretation.

The importance of the sages for rabbinic literature and its transmission can hardly be overestimated. We have already noted that by the time Daniel, Esther, and Ruth were composed, the sages had become a powerful voice for the interpretation and transmission of Torah and Prophets. The importance of the rabbis is therefore a logical continuation of this development, as Hanson has recently noted.

> [The sages] were heirs to the stream of tradition stemming from the Priestly Writing, the reform of Ezra and Nehemiah, the Chronicler's

History, and the community ideals and piety reflected in Sirach. . . . For
the sapiential concern with ordering the diverse phenomena of the
everyday world into one perfect unity became a powerful ally in the
rabbi's efforts to draw all aspects of life into the order of reality revealed
by God in the Torah.[30]

If, however, we may see continuity between the sages and scribes
of the post-exilic and rabbinic periods, we also find a new development
regarding the stature of the sages that will have far-reaching implications for the nature of scripture. The distinction between sages and
scribes became clearer, with the former given more status and power
within the community and the latter becoming essentially copyists.[31]
With the increasing importance of the literature of the sages came a
need to affirm the authority of these figures in a more explicit way;
that is, as the responses to Torah and Prophets became authoritative
and carried as much normative weight as the written scripture, some
way had to be found to connect and ground that authority and the
writings of the rabbis themselves in scriptural authority.

The solution to this problem—at once occasioned by logical continuity of the interpretive process begun in the Writings and yet moving
far beyond the role and status of these authors—was found in the
notion of a twofold Torah, oral and written.

That doctrine of the dual Torah, that is of the Torah in two media, came
about in response to the problem of explaining the standing and authority
of the Mishnah. But the broadening of the symbol of the Torah first took
shape around the figure of the sage. That symbolism accounted for the
sages' authority. Only later on, in the fourth century, in the pages of the
Yerushalaim, did the doctrine of the dual Torah reach expression. . . .
What the sages said formed a chain of tradition extending back to Sinai.
Hence it was equivalent to the Torah. The upshot is that words of sages
enjoyed the status of the Torah. The small step beyond, I think, was to
claim that what sages said was Torah, *as much as what Scripture said
was Torah.*[32]

The historical implications of such a view of Torah, namely, that
from Sinai on there was Oral and Written Torah, are generally dis-
counted.[33] Nevertheless, this doctrine does tell us much about the
heightened role of the sage in rabbinic literature and the coalescing
of scripture, interpretation, and the contemporary giver of interpretation, the sage or rabbi.

Scripture, the Mishnah, the sage—all three spoke with equal authority.
True, one thing had to come in alignment with the other, the Mishnah

with Scripture, the sage with Mishnah. . . . Interpretation and what was interpreted, exegesis and text, belonged together . . . the rabbi's book, whether Talmud to the Mishnah or *midrash* to scripture, is *torah,* that is, revealed by God . . . the rabbi is like Moses, "our rabbi," who received *torah* and wrote the Torah. . . . So in the rabbi, the word of God was made flesh.[34]

We have come a long way from the Writings and their notion of scripture, to be sure. However, the interpretive process and the role of the sage found there provide continuity with subsequent developments.

Although the diversity of the interpretation and setting in rabbinic literature makes summarizations about the nature of Judaism subject to debate, E. P. Sanders has found a general pattern that provides us with a point of departure for comparing this literature with the Writings.

The pattern is this: God has chosen Israel and Israel has accepted the election. In his role as King, God gave Israel commandments which they are to obey as best they can. Obedience is rewarded and disobedience punished. In case of failure to obey, however, man has recourse to divinely ordained means of atonement, in all of which repentance is required. As long as he maintains his desire to stay in the covenant he has a share in God's covenantal promises, including life in the world to come. The intention and effort to be obedient constitute the *condition for remaining in the covenant,* but they do not *earn* it.[35]

Some general points of comparison with the literature of the Writings and this pattern are now in order. First, to the extent this pattern is valid, we may see that the retributional system found in Torah (especially Deuteronomy), Chronicles, the scribal tradition, and much of the liturgical literature is central to what follows. Continuity with the increasing concern with repentance is already reflected in the Psalms and Ezra–Nehemiah. Obedience to the Law, so important in much of the Writings and intertestamental literature, also represents a point of continuity.

But where are the Prophets? Here Sanders has been criticized for providing too narrow a pattern, although he has argued that the apocalyptic literature, for example, does not represent a different pattern. Whether or not apocalyptic literature and other intertestamental and New Testament literature fit into the pattern described by Sanders, it seems clear that much of the early rabbinic writing that became Mishnah has its primary focus on Torah and not the Prophets. Even here, however, we must proceed with caution, for the open-endedness of the written Torah itself and the prophetic influences upon, for example, 1–2 Chronicles, which also are governed by a retributional theological system, must be kept in mind. If, however, Torah is central to the early rabbis, the tension between Torah and Prophets is not lost; indeed, it manifests itself in the later (Amoraim) additions to the Mishnah that ultimately make up a part of the Talmud. Neusner has recently argued that the Messiah becomes important for these post-mishnaic rabbis, partially because of the need to deal with this unfulfilled dimension of the scriptural message and partially because of the adverse conditions of the people.[36] The incorporation of messianic thought into the Mishnah does not result in apocalyptic visions and expectations, however. Rather, as in Christianity, the figure of the Messiah to come is a figure of stability in a world that still awaits its ultimate fulfillment. "The Talmud's version of the Messiah became what the sages of Mishnah and its continuators most needed: a rabbi-Messiah, who would save an Israel sanctified through Torah."[37] The subsequent developments of rabbinic thought transform the notion of Messianic thought found in the Prophets. This had also occurred in other ways in the Writings. Such developments preserve and reflect the tension that all Torah-Prophets communities must have between the already and the not yet, between a focus on the needs and concerns of the present and the hopes for a different future.

As with the New Testament literature, the rabbinic literature does not easily fit into the categories we have used to compare and contrast the Writings with intertestamental literature, despite many common concerns and places where continuity is present. Again, as with the New Testament, the rabbinic literature represents different and new genres or types of interpretation. Nevertheless, the Haggadah does have parallels with the edifying and sapiential literature of the Writings. Moreover, the Halachah has concerns in common with Ezra–Nehemiah, 1–2 Chronicles, and sapiential and liturgical literature. The tension between Torah and Prophets, the centrality of Torah, the need to interpret the scriptures in light of new needs and different circumstances—all of this coming from a necessary interaction between a people and its "book"—this is the heritage of the Writings for the rabbinic literature. Like the New Testament, the Writings are in one sense invisible. To be sure, they are mentioned frequently and are interpreted, but their primary value for understanding this literature is in the process they begin and upon which the later sages are dependent. That process ultimately, for Jews and Christians, results in quite different canons. Without the Writings and their interpretive paradigms, however, we are at a loss to see both what is shared and what is different.

The diversity of rabbinic literature and its relationship to the scriptural canon, analogous to the New Testament writings, might look something like this, with the Writings as a critical connecting link between the two major components.[38]

CANON REVISITED

In our examination of the vast intertestamental, Christian, and rabbinic literature from the period 200 B.C.E. to 200 C.E. and later, we have found both continuity and consensus, and diversity and divergence with the Writings. Much of this literature can be seen to be contingent upon developments begun in the Writings. To the communities that produced and utilized them, much of this textual material must also be seen as specific and particular responses to new situations that confronted and challenged Jewish and Christian communities.

One significant factor in this period that has been discussed only briefly to this point is the stabilization of scripture: the fact that lines were being drawn to delimit the shape of the scriptural writings. Our interest here is primarily with the Hebrew Bible, Tanak. More specifically, we wish to address the question of how our study of the Writings contributes resolution to the debates over the formation and function of the Hebrew Bible.

The continuity and discontinuity found between the Writings and the literature that follows it testified to the importance of Torah and Prophets. In New Testament literature, the influence of the Prophets appears to be primary—not surprising for communities that have experienced the coming of the Messiah. In the rabbinic literature, the Torah appears to hold central importance. In both literatures, however, the whole of Torah and Prophets and the tensions between them is not lost. As in the case of Ecclesiasticus, the New Testament reflects a knowledge of a tripartite canon, although the extent and nature of the third division remains cloudy. Such is not the case for the rabbinic literature, which clearly, and from a later period, reflects a scripture including all of the books in the Writings. Although none of the literature we have studied provides us with clear evidence for the time of canonization or the details of the process that finally produced the Writings, nevertheless, it is generally accepted that the Hebrew canon in its present form (Tanak) was a matter of consensus by the end of the first century C.E.

One piece of corroborative evidence for this dating is the result of our comparisons made with intertestamental, New Testament, and rabbinic literature. Although the intertestamental literature corresponds at least loosely with the types of literature found in the Writings, the New Testament and rabbinic literature by and large do not. Why should this be the case? To stress the particularity in experience of each literature and its communities does not satisfactorily explain this difference. Although surely those who confess Jesus as the Christ and those governed by rabbinical structures inevitably produce different literature, the incongruity of this literature with the Writings and intertestamental literature does not remain fully explained. It is proposed here that the notion of *canon, not scripture,* may aid us here; that is, as Torah, Prophets, and the Writings become normative and fixed, responses to them take on a different character and purpose. Scripture is growing into canon, or into something very close to it. Surely the Christians and Jews of the first century C.E. continue to produce literature that is "like" the Writings and that, with the New Testament literature, can in one sense be seen as continued "writings" in an open canon. However, for much of New Testament and virtually all of the rabbinic literature, the differences in form (e.g., gospels, epistles, midrash, mishnah, etc.) point toward a commentary upon a fixed, normative, and stable body of literature. The fact that there are diverse responses, including many intertestamental ones from the same period, reflects the pluralism of scripture, now made concrete in a canon. The fact that the New Testament itself is actually a composite of many responses merely affirms this point.

If canon is a concept that should be used in this period, we must still address the issue of whether and when such a canon was "closed." It must be noted here that the question of whether the canon was "open" or "closed" during this period is a different, if related, question from that of whether the Hebrew canon was stabilized by the end of the first century C.E. Many have argued that the Hebrew canon reached its present form long before the New Testament period.[39] If we accept this view, the canon was stable and closed quite early. The evidence for such a view depends on later sources, including the New Testament and Josephus, for corroboration.

Others have argued that the intertestamental literature and the New Testament literature reflect situations when the canon was still open to additions, further authoritative commentary, and interpretation, which themselves were capable of becoming a part of scripture. When this later literature is compared with the Writings, no clear answer to the open or closed status of canon emerges. On the one hand, the intertestamental literature and the New Testament reflect situations in which a stabilized text—for Torah, Prophets, and much of the Writings—exists. On the other hand, this literature also represents responses to scripture that have continuity with the Writings and may point to an open canon. Brevard Childs has clearly stated the issue relative to the New Testament literature.

> Did the canon of the New Testament develop in analogy to an Old Testament process which had largely reached its goal of stabilization before the New Testament period, or rather did the major canonical force stem from the side of the Christian church which resulted in the definition of the Jewish Scriptures as an Old Testament within the larger Christian Bible?[40]

To pose a similar question for Judaism, we could substitute "Talmud" or some other designation for the subsequent, authoritative rabbinic tradition. In either case, for Christians or Jews, the question is difficult to answer because we are often dependent upon later conceptions and descriptions of the canon. Our tentative answer is yes and no. Yes, the late post-exilic period, the intertestamental literature, the New Testament, and the rabbinic material reflect a fairly stable scripture of Torah, Prophets, and Writings. No, this same literature (perhaps omitting the rabbinic literature) seems to be explained best by the concept of an open canon with many analogies and parallels between the Writings.

Two other observations are pertinent here. First, the Septuagint has often been important in discussing the issue of canon. For a long time it was suggested that this Greek translation of Torah and Prophets, which also contains much additional material not found in the Hebrew Bible, represented a different, "Alexandrian" canon. Recently, however, scholarly opinion has swung toward the view that a different canon was never functional for Judaism, that the Jewish canon was open until a later period.[41] Although the issues raised by the Septuagint cannot be resolved here, it should be noted that this collection of writings,

with a different order and some literature different from the Hebrew
Bible, affirms the role and nature of scripture and the Writings set
forth above; that is, although Torah and Prophets are of central import
to post-exilic Judaism, the rest is in flux. Based on the evidence of the
Septuagint, this flux would appear to be found not simply in the
particular books associated with Torah and Prophets, but also with the
order, or collection process. Again, our suggestion that we have a
stable but open canon best explains the diversity and the central place
of Torah found in the Septuagint.

Finally, we must consider a recent, and fairly radical, argument for
an open canon by Jacob Neusner.

> We must now wonder whether, any longer, we can distinguish between
> *torah,* as divine revelation, and "the canon of the Torah," a particular
> set of books deemed more authoritative than any other books. If what
> our authorized rabbi states must be received as *torah,* as divine reve-
> lation, then we face two possibilities. Either there is *torah* which is not
> part of the Torah, the canon of revelation. Or there is no such thing as
> a canon at all. . . . The entire thrust of the exegetical process is to link
> upon a single plane of authority and reliability what a rabbi now says
> with what the (written) Torah said, what the Mishnah says with what
> the (written) Torah said. . . .
> God spoke in various ways and through diverse media: to prophets
> and to sages, in writing and in memorized sayings, to olden times and
> to the present day. We can discern no systematic effort to distinguish
> one kind of revelation from another—revelation transmitted in writings,
> that transmitted orally, revelation to an ancient prophet, an exegesis or
> a Torah-teaching of a contemporary sage.[42]

On the one hand, we agree with this assessment, for two reasons.
First, such a view affirms the continuation of the process of authoritative commentary begun in the Writings. A case could be made for
this process beginning at Sinai (Oral Tradition?) and, in this sense,
everything from Moses to the present day has the possibility of being
received and accepted as authoritative. Second, such a view is compatible with, for example, a notion of scripture and tradition that places
as much, if not more, authority upon the latter as the former. This
would appear to be the case for many if not most Christian and Jewish
communities today.

On the other hand, we must disagree with this statement. Regardless
of the question of authority, distinctions are made between the Scriptures and subsequent teachings of sages, bishops, reformers, and others.
Thus, the notion of a canon as a closed body of authoritative writings,

although not necessarily more authoritative than other writings or new revelations of God in various forms, is functional for the scriptural communities of Christians and Jews.

The Writings themselves constitute part of the problem and also contribute to its solution. They initiate a process of interpretation, continued into the subsequent literature of Jews and Christians. In a sense, that process never ends, thus raising the question of the inter-relationship between scripture and tradition and the value of a notion of canon. Yet, we have maintained that the Writings clearly testify to the presence of Torah and Prophets in the post-exilic period and to the need for many different communities to make response to a common, written, authoritative corpus. Although the relationship, from the perspective of authority, between the "book" and the interpretation can be different for particular communities, the distinction between them is clear and warrants the use of canon to describe the stability of one part of the written tradition. Thus, Christians may forget or ignore or consciously reject Thomas Aquinas or Martin Luther, and Jews may likewise fail to consider Ibn Ezra or even Maimonides, but contemporary sages must always pay at least lip service to the written "canons" to which these later sages and interpreters referred.

We conclude this study of the Writings and the literature that followed it by noting an important parallel between Jesus and the rabbinic sages. In both cases the communities of faith that followed their lead saw them as authoritative interpreters and enactors of Torah and Prophets. As such, Jesus and the sages both reflect a continuation of the process begun in the Writings. They are heirs of Ezra, Nehemiah, the early sages and scribes, the psalmists, and others. Like the authors and heroes of the Writings, their lives and teachings become authoritative for subsequent communities. Unlike their predecessors, however, the values and subsequent "doctrines" associated with them become constitutive of a diversity that can no longer be embraced by all scriptural communities of faith. Rather, the hermeneutics or interpretations of Torah and Prophets develop in quite different directions and finally result in different scriptural canons, as well as communities with different missions and identities. Our purpose in this study has not been to stress the differences, however, but the common roots that both canonical communities share. The Writings set in motion a process that can explain and account for diversity and even animosity. The Writings also represent what was shared by all communities in the intertestamental, New Testament, and rabbinic periods. It also represents what can be shared by contemporary Christians and Jews, as it was by Jesus and the sages.

6

The Writings
as Canon

The value of studying the Writings as a response to Torah and Prophets in the post-exilic period is at least twofold. First, the responses reflected by this literature present some of the priorities (e.g., worship, community establishment) that early Judaism saw as important for the continuing life of post-exilic Israel. Many of these responses came to have a paradigmatic function for subsequent scriptural communities. For example, the centrality of Torah, the emphasis upon repentance, the authoritative role of the sage—these developments became priorities for future communities. They reflect not simply the needs of post-exilic communities but the needs of future communities as well. Second, the Writings represent a process of dialogue between community and text that became constitutive for all communities. That dialogue, continuing into later periods, ultimately caused two different canonical communities to be formed.

At some point during this period, the Writings themselves become scripture and, finally, become a part of a fixed canon. Although the evidence from the intertestamental and New Testament literature should caution us against presupposing a fixed canon with no flexibility, it also witnesses to the authoritative role and function of much of the Writings (e.g., Psalms). The majority of scholars who attempt to fix the time of canonization for the Hebrew Bible in its present form (Torah-Prophets-Writings) suggest dates somewhere between 200 B.C.E. and 100 C.E. I have suggested above that a later rather than an earlier date is more congruent with the textual evidence, although I do not wish to engage in extended discussion or debate with students of the history of canon. Rather, I want, on the one hand, to affirm the difficulty of determining precisely when the canon was formed and when it was generally accepted in the shape it presently has. On the other hand, I want to acknowledge that canonization of the Hebrew

Bible—the determination of all the literature to be contained therein—did occur in this period. My concern in this chapter is not to comment upon the process that effected this development but rather to explore the results and implications of such a development for the way in which scripture functions as a canon now.

When scripture, and in particular the Writings, becomes part of a fixed canon, certain changes occur both in the way this literature is perceived by the community of faith and in the way it is used. To this point our study has had a historical concern; that is, we have tried to show how Torah and Prophets were perceived and used by particular communities. When these historical responses become a part of a scriptural canon, however, their historical particularity becomes in one way less important. It is necessary not only to see the Writings as historical response but also to ask how this diverse literature functions as scripture within a closed canon.

Reading the Writings as canon rather than as diverse post-exilic books is to become immersed in a different level of meaning. At the canonical level there are several internal changes of focus or concern within the Writings. Some of these are consonant with the intentions of the post-exilic communities that produced them. Yet, some changes represent discontinuity: uses and meanings that were not a part of the original communities' concerns.

One significant change effected by the canon is the relationship of history, text, and community of faith. This represents a perennial hermeneutical problem. How do we relate a text speaking out of and to a particular historical community to another completely different historical community? It is suggested here that the canon, by creating a boundary around the ancient text, also creates the problem. The relating of ancient scripture to the contemporary community is not to be done primarily by a series of interlocking historical commentaries to which the community of faith refers. Rather, this is done anew, with each generation first experiencing a sort of culture shock in interaction with the ancient biblical text and then developing ways and means to explicate its meaning.

Precisely at this point, the historical background of these texts sometimes takes on less importance. History is surely not irrelevant, for the shape of the books themselves can be explained only in light of careful historical research. However, our history is the history that now engages the text, not, for example, Ezra's, however important Ezra's history may have been for shaping the "original" text. Moreover, the canonical context (structure-limits-shape) suggests that we do not need to be in the situation of a restoration community in order to be convinced of the Torah's importance for structuring and regulating our own community of faith. Surely the author of Ezra–Nehemiah would be pleased with such a function for this literature, but this is part of the canon and not as part of the original book. Scripture in its canonical form is now available to all communities of faith, regardless of how much or how little historical research they have done.

The diversity of response to scripture found in the Writings and in the subsequent literature produced by Christians and Jews is, I have suggested, the result of both the particular situations that confronted these communities and the pluralism found in Torah and Prophets. When the Writings become a part of the canon, the pluralism of scripture is expanded and sharpened; the diversity of response reflected in this literature becomes normative. On the one hand, we can speak of a pluralism—cultural and scriptural in nature—in the communities that originally produced the Writings only with many qualifications and reservations. On the other hand, when the Writings are seen as canon, pluralism is characteristic not simply of Torah and Prophets but also of all scripture. It is the effects of such a canonical phenomenon that we wish to explore in this chapter.

Perhaps the most significant function of the Writings as canon is not the particular paradigms of interpretation or priorities they present but the process of interaction between text and community to which they witness. Regardless of new methods, perspectives, and needs of a community that motivate new interpretations and applications of the scriptural message, the essential factor—the indispensable characteristic of a scriptural community—is a dialogue between text and community. The Writings witness to and make normative such a dialogue. In this sense the Writings initiate the starting point for a continuum of scriptural interpretation that provides identity and direction for all subsequent communities that have Torah and Prophets as scripture.

In the remainder of this chapter, we will explore the canonical function of the Writings as it relates to four different aspects of this dialogue between community and text. First, the nature of canon and pluralism will be studied. Then, the relationships of canon to (1) the *texts* of the Writings; and (2) the *communities* that use the Writings will be investigated. Third, the significance of the Writings for understanding a twofold (Old Testament–New Testament; Tanak-Talmud) pattern of scripture for Christianity and Judaism will be discussed. Finally, a look at some of the ways in which the Writings function in their diversity and as a synthetic whole, a canonical collection, will conclude this chapter.

CANON AND PLURALISM

Throughout this study we have referred to and used the concept of pluralism in three different ways. First, the Diaspora provides the context for cultural pluralism. The existence of many communities of faith in different cultures creates this type of pluralism. The common matrix that binds these communities together is the affirmation that they are all a part of Israel, God's people, wherever they are living. Speaking of a unity of mission or purpose for these communities is difficult, however, for the diversity of their circumstances in the early post-exilic period produces different priorities and affirms different values. Living apart from each other as Israel would probably be easier than living together. Such cultural pluralism is also reflected in the early Christian communities.[1]

Second, we may also speak of religious pluralism in the period. Here we refer to the existence of several different religious communities (Greek, Roman, Jewish, Christian, etc.) within one state or politically controlled territory. Religious pluralism is possible only when the state is able to transcend the interests of one religion and allow several religions to exist at once. The common matrix of this pluralism is the state itself. There is always a tension in such a situation, then or now, for the political interests of many religions push toward making their particular truth *the* truth of the state and of the entire culture.

Third and most important, we have found a scriptural pluralism. The matrix of scriptural pluralism is the scripture, Torah and Prophets, which is both the common property of the post-exilic communities and that which generates diverse responses, by its multivalent nature and the tensions inherent within it.

As a result of the collection of Torah, Prophets, and Writings into one canon, we may now speak of a fourth type of pluralism, canonical pluralism. To speak of the canon as a common matrix for all scriptural communities is first to broaden the literature that is common and authoritative to all. Ultimately, of course, canonical pluralism will need to be defined and broadened to include the New Testament for Christians and many rabbinic writings for Jews, but our concern here is first with the Writings. The inclusion of the Writings in the scriptural canon continues to affirm the centrality of Torah and Prophets. Because these post-exilic responses point to Torah and Prophets, the conservative nature of scriptural pluralism is preserved.

When the Writings become scripture, a fundamental change occurs, one that justifies the distinction between scriptural and canonical pluralism. Now the diversity of response and interpretation found in the Writings is sanctioned not by the cultures in which scriptural communities are found, nor by the historical circumstances and priorities of particular communities. Rather, the pluralism of the Writings, however it was produced, is sanctioned by the canon itself. Thus, the canon expands the nature of scriptural pluralism because it sanctions a diversity of interpretation and response to Torah and Prophets "originally" possible only because of different communities' cultural settings. The pluralism of the canon is now the common property of all communities of faith, whether they like it or not. Historically, it is difficult to believe that apocalyptic seers and the community builders of Ezra–Nehemiah could have lived together easily. In the canon, however, these and other diverse responses do live together—creating a challenge and corrective to each other and to later interpreters and enactors of Torah and Prophets.

The pluralistic nature of the Writings, which becomes a blueprint for understanding and sanctioning the development of both Judaism and Christianity, contains continuities and discontinuities. On the one hand, the individual books, understood as representative of particular approaches and concerns found within the scriptural community, can be seen to exercise similar functions at all times. The call for centrality of Torah in Ezra–Nehemiah, the paradigmatic prayers of the Psalms, and the reason-oriented approach to experience in Proverbs, all of these representing stable functions of this literature in every period. On the other hand, viewing *all* the Writings, with their own agendas and vested interests, as part of a pluralistic response to Torah and Prophets is to run counter to their original nonpluralistic intentions. For example, to understand Ezra–Nehemiah and Daniel as equally legitimate options for a basis of belief and social structures is surely to go beyond the particular intentions of either. This function of discontinuity within the canon is a crucial one if diversity within a pluralistic matrix, however defined, is to be affirmed as valuable in the contemporary faith community. Issues of church unity, ecumenism, and interfaith dialogue are at stake here; the canon may be of help. The ultimate value of the Writings and this concept of canonical pluralism lie in their ability to transcend the particularity of any given scriptural paradigm or interpretation. On the one hand, the Writings point us to the Torah-Prophets. On the other hand, they legitimate diversity, calling us to listen to voices we might normally choose to ignore.

CANON AND TEXT

The Writings are the result of a dialogue between the written scripture of early Judaism and the needs of different communities attempting to understand the actions and will of the God of Israel. When the Writings of the Hebrew Bible become scripture, a tripartite division of the canon is created. The following three sections of this chapter seek to explore the effects of this three-part canonical division on the role and function of the originally diverse responses of the Writings, which are now a part of the scriptures. The effect of canonization on the texts of the Writings is our first concern.

Using the dialogue between text and community as a way of conceptualizing the role of the Writings, the following picture is suggested:

Torah and Prophets ⟷ Writings
Text ⟷ Community

Although such a picture has been used to describe the historical developments in the Writings, our concern here is with the Writings as scripture and part of canon. Two important points of continuity between the literature of the Writings viewed as particular historical responses to scripture and as a part of the canon should be remembered. The first point of continuity is that the Writings are always referential in nature. That is, they point to other, more fundamental scripture. They are not complete messages; they need Torah and Prophets to make sense. Their use of the traditions and concerns of Torah and Prophets presupposes communities who know these scriptures and who want and need to appropriate their teachings. They presuppose the authority of Torah and Prophets, without which the message of the Writings is ineffectual. The second point of continuity between the Writings as post-exilic literature and as scripture is their diversity. Regardless of the fact that all of the Writings are now seen as authoritative scripture, the differences between their messages remains a basic characteristic of this literature.

If the referential nature and the diversity of the Writings remain unchanged by their inclusion within the scriptural canon, the nature of this literature and its use by subsequent scriptural communities are affected. When this diverse literature becomes a part of scripture authoritative for all communities, these communities are being told, in effect, that wisdom thinking, liturgical living, and establishment concerns are all a part of what it means to be the people of God. In the post-exilic period we can well conceive that the response of Ezra–Nehemiah was dismissed by certain communities far from Jerusalem. When Ezra–Nehemiah becomes scripture and a part of the canon, however, the canon itself prevents a facile dismissal of this literature. Surely subsequent Christian and Jewish communities will interpret Torah and Prophets in ways sometimes antithetical to, for example, Ezra–Nehemiah; nevertheless, they will also be judged by a canonical yardstick that includes this literature. The effect of placing the literature of the Writings in the canon is to provide the community of faith with several diverse interpretations and sets of priorities that give much greater freedom, on the one hand, and continually remind the community of other options, also scriptural, on the other. A brief overview of this development for the five types of literature we have found in the Writings is now in order.

Despite the fact that the sages become a dominant factor in the transmission of scripture, the sapiential literature of the Writings has often created difficulty for scriptural communities because of its different form and content and because of the problem of relating its message to the more normative message of Torah and Prophets. This difficulty is in one way increased when the sapiential literature is a part of the canon, for now this way of speaking and thinking is built into the structure of what it means to be a scriptural community. In another way, however, the pertinence and applicability of this literature to other scripture is increased. Now, for example, we do not have to read Ecclesiasticus to equate Torah with the wisdom of God—the canon does this for us. Proverbs 8 must be related to Torah, and Proverbs 2 must be related to the Prophets, regardless of the intentions of "original" authors. Moreover, we need not, we should not, try to identify the "wise" with one particular social setting, because as scripture this literature belongs to all within the community. Although this literature still retains an upper class or establishment bias, it can be used by the poor and the disenfranchised to claim some of the rights and privileges of wise living for themselves. The critical questioning of the order of this world, the justice of God, found in Job, Ecclesiastes, and parts of Proverbs is no longer the response of a few dissident sages; it should characterize the entire community of faith. The sapiential literature with its hard questions, its affirmation of a common-sense approach to life, its belief in a created order, its central concern for education—this is the property of all.

The liturgical literature undergoes an equally significant transformation when it becomes scripture. No longer are we able to dismiss the "later" psalms of Torah-oriented sages and singers as inferior or less important. The Torah structure of the Psalms, provided so late in the process of their composition, now demands that we relate these originally disparate prayers to the central scripture of the community. The particularity of these prayers remains an essential part of their message, but as canon they now function to remind us that lamentation, wisdom meditation, repentance, and praise are mandated for the entire community regardless of where on the spectrum of spiritual journey we find ourselves. Although we can and will identify with some of these psalms more than others, none of them is irrelevant; they have all become God's authoritative word to us. To cite one example, the lament psalms cannot be dismissed. Too often we wish in worship to forget or avoid the problems that confront us. Even in good times, these psalms serve to remind us that all is not well, and that God must be directly addressed, even confronted, in the light of our imperfect world. Likewise, when our world is falling apart, Psalms reminds us that our final word to God, and from God, will be praise, even if achieved only through lamentation. Thus, the liturgical literature, in its particularity, in its demand to relate the promises of old to the present situation of the community and the world, in its multivalent character—in its call to study, to lament, to give thanks, to praise—provides the contours for meaningful and appropriate worship within a community that has scripture at its center. Although time will change our priorities and create new problems, the responses called for by this literature remain constant.

The historical literature of the Writings provides a challenge when viewed as a part of the scriptural canon. All too often we wish to dismiss its establishment bias and the demand for orthodoxy represented here. Yet, the building up of the community of faith, the need for an authoritative center, the need to relate the problems of the worshiping community to larger political events and powers—all of these must be addressed by the community. Although our answers may not be Ezra's answers, the scriptural force of this literature does not let us forget these needs. If a scriptural community chooses at times to look beyond itself and its internal needs, this literature suggests a corrective may be needed. The historical literature also provides us with a mandate to relate the scriptural stories and their values to our contemporary story. The books of 1–2 Chronicles and Ezra–Nehemiah witness to an activity that must characterize all scriptural communities: the retelling of the scriptural story in light of contemporary events. Through such an activity the law of Moses, the faith of Abraham, and the activities of David become and remain central to the life of the communities that follow their lead.

The edifying literature of Ruth, Esther, and Daniel (1—6) takes on new functions for the community when it is a part of the canon. No longer may they be seen as simply the stories of particular communities in the post-exilic period. Rather, they witness to the continuing need for paradigms of behavior in times of trouble. They point all subsequent communities to the crucial role of scripture in providing identity (Esther), direction (Daniel), and witnessing to ultimate restoration (Esther and Ruth). Moreover, these stories require the communities that succeed them to find other examples and means of living faithfully, to create new stories that will serve as examples and illustrations of God's guidance in the world.

The inclusion of apocalyptic literature in the Hebrew canon creates continuity and discontinuity for the scriptural community. On the one hand, this literature points us backward to Torah and the Prophets, to unfulfilled promises and a fallen world, which God will still act to save. As such, this literature is compatible with the open-endedness of Torah and the still unfulfilled words of the prophets. On the other hand, this literature pushes beyond the scripture to new revelations and new ways in which God's will is to be known, to new ways in which God will act. In this sense, apocalyptic literature prevents the community from too much reliance upon the here and now and upon the efficacy of our actions for ultimate transformation of this world into the kingdom of God. Like all the literature of the Writings, apocalyptic literature is now the property of all; it is not simply the message of the disenfranchised and oppressed few who dream of better times. Now the vision of the end is an inescapable part of all scriptural communities.

Brevard Childs has described the formation of canon in the following way:

> A religious reading of Israel's tradition arose early in its history and extended in different ways throughout the oral, literary, and redactional stages in the growth of the material until it reached a final form of relative stability. The process did not happen all at once; there was no one

overarching hermeneutic to realize the goal; some attempts were more successful than others.[2]

The Writings, together with Torah and Prophets, represent the "successful" readings of Israel's tradition, as reflected by their inclusion in the Hebrew canon. Even though we will probably never know precisely why this literature and not other literature was successful, the effect of this success transformed the particular responses they reflect into general concerns and priorities that became authoritative for all subsequent Jewish and Christian communities. As such, they function to make all of us potential sages, singers, community builders, and apocalyptic seers. Should we admit that we cannot be all of these at once, nevertheless, we will be called to account—through the authority of the Writings and those communities that hold them as scripture—by others who represent the interpretive perspectives we have forgotten or chosen to ignore.

CANON AND COMMUNITY

Our observations about the nature of the Writings as canon present a problem for the community of faith: No one community is capable of affirming and living out all of the priorities found in the Writings. To be sure, this problem can be dealt with by suggesting that because different communities will choose different priorities and models, it is the interaction between all scriptural communities that keeps them honest and also maintains the validity of any particular interpretation of Torah and Prophets based upon the Writings. Yet, this does not solve the problem for the particular community confronted by the diversity of this literature. How does a community choose from the options available? How does a community relate its own notion of mission to all of the tradition? Although such problems include all aspects of the community-text interrelationship, the literature of the Writings does present the problem clearly.

To this point we have concentrated on the textual dimension of the dialogue between text and community that produced the Writings and that continues into the present day. In this section we wish to examine the community dimension of this dialogue. The following schematic reflects one way of describing this dialogue.

1. Text ⟷ Community
2. Torah-Prophets-Writings ⟷ Contemporary Needs and Events

In this picture the Writings represent not the needs of the community, but rather a text that must be related to those needs. It is presupposed that although those needs are to be found in new problems and events, the community's perception of them and their relationship to the Writings will be colored by Torah and Prophets. The community is challenged by the diversity of the Writings and the need to apply their messages.

The history of Christianity and Judaism is replete with different approaches to the problem of diversity in scripture. Its solution is always dependent upon factors extrinsic to the biblical text and particular to specific communities. With this observation and qualification in mind, we wish to illustrate both the need to make sense of scriptural diversity and one solution to the problem as an illustration of the community side of the text-community dialogue. Our example is the Megilloth, a subcanonical division of the Writings. The Megilloth ("scrolls") is a collection of five books: the Song of Songs, Ruth, Lamentations, Ecclesiastes, and Esther. These books appear to have been placed together in the Hebrew canon since the sixth century C.E. Their order in the manuscripts is varied, sometimes depending upon a historical (by author [e.g., Solomon] or time [e.g., Ruth]) rationale, at other times by their use within the liturgical year. Regardless of their order, the collection derives its ultimate rationale from the liturgical reading of these books at five major occasions in the year: Song of Songs (Passover); Ruth (Weeks); Lamentations (Ninth of Ab); Ecclesiastes (Booths); and Esther (Purim).

Several observations about the Megilloth are in order. First, this collection represents a *postcanonical* activity on the part of Judaism. Second, this collection stems from the needs and desires of the contemporary community to organize its scripture. Third, this collection goes well beyond the intentions of the original books, although the pertinence of Esther and Lamentations for the occasions on which they are read is clear. Fourth, there is no attempt to provide a representative picture of all the literature in the Writings; the community simply uses what it perceives as appropriate to the occasion and does not worry about what is left out.

If we cannot provide answers to why these five books and not others were chosen, the reason for a collection at all seems clear enough. The Megilloth "derives from the need for a systematic arrangement."[3] Although we can envision several other circumstances that might also motivate such a collection process, the worship life of the contemporary, postcanonical community creates a need for the diversity of scripture, in particular the Writings, to be organized, even systematized. Such a collection makes sense of diverse and originally unrelated literature, uses it, and enables the community to appropriate its canon in a special way. Although the Megilloth is not a functional canonical unit for Christians, it reflects the needs of all Christians and Jews to make sense of their scripture, to organize it according to their contemporary needs—needs partially grounded in the scriptures themselves.

The Bible may be seen as diverse literature filled with many different books, much as an orchestra contains many different instruments. From time to time different books will be chosen to play particular pieces of music, to meet special needs of the entire community. The five books of the Megilloth represent such a special need. Originally they were five separate books in the post-exilic period. In the Septuagint these books are associated with wisdom and poetry (Ecclesiastes and the Song of Songs); history (Esther and sometimes Ruth); liturgical literature (Ruth, because of the connection with David); and the Prophets (Lamentations). Ultimately, at a much later date, these books are brought together in the Hebrew Bible. They are related to each other on the basis of contemporary needs, the worship of a later time, but even here there is continuity with the scriptural dynamic of text and community found within the scriptures themselves. The following schematic reflects this:

Megilloth ◄──────────► Contemporary Worship
Text ◄──────────► Community

The dialogue between text and community reflected in the Megilloth is found throughout the history of Christian and Jewish communities. Lectionary cycles are but one more example of such a dialogue, with the primary organization of such cycles dependent on *both* the structure of the canon *and* the contemporary needs of the community. If the Writings present the community with a problem, namely, diversity, they also witness to a dialogue between scripture and community that is capable of solving the problem because it can provide systems or organization that will meet contemporary needs and continue the life of the scriptural community.

THE TWOFOLD SCRIPTURES OF JUDAISM AND CHRISTIANITY

To this point we have focused upon the Writings and their relationship to Torah and Prophets in the canon of the Hebrew Bible. However important such a relationship is for understanding the nature and function of the Writings and of the Hebrew Bible or Old Testament, it is ultimately an incomplete picture of canon. Both Christianity and Judaism have larger authoritative canons: the Old Testament and New Testament for Christians; the Hebrew Bible (Tanak), the Talmud (Mishnah and Gemarah), and other rabbinic literature for Jews. Here we will relate our study of the Writings as post-exilic responses to Torah and Prophets and as a canonical collection of scripture to the larger authoritative bodies of literature of which they are a part. Our primary concern is to answer the question, How do the Writings help us understand the shape and function of scripture and canon for Christians and Jews?

As in our study of the Writings themselves, the process of dialogue between text and community is critical for understanding the ultimate shape of Christian and Jewish canons. Such a dialogue takes seriously both the stories and stipulations of the old and the new events that the community of faith experiences. This dialogue continues into the present day, and the following schematic illustrates this ongoing process.

Old ◄─────────► New
Text ◄─────────► Community

We wish to present a historical overview of this process. While our attention is focused on the literature that became authoritative for later generations of Christians and Jews, the contributions of other writers and communities discussed in the preceding chapter need to be kept in mind. This other literature reflects the same text-community process and provides important examples of what it means to be a scriptural community wrestling with new revelation and new demands.

We may begin with an example of the text-community dialogue found in Torah itself. Leaving aside the historical and source-critical questions of whether we should speak of an "original" Tetrateuch (Genesis through Numbers), Pentateuch (Genesis through Deuteronomy), or Hexateuch (Genesis through Joshua), one way of viewing Torah is to separate the stories and laws found in Genesis through Numbers from the farewell speech (or testament?) of Moses found in Deuteronomy. In this last book of the Torah, Moses reviews the history of Israel up to that moment and provides a "new" collection of law that represents present concerns and some reinterpretation of old laws. All of this is done with the understanding that entry into the promised land will call for both obedience to the law and some adaptation and new application of that law in light of new circumstances. Whether we view Deuteronomy as a part of the "old" story (Genesis through Numbers) or as a seventh-century reform document in the time of Josiah, the pattern remains the same: Moses is reinterpreting the law in light both of the people's past story and of the future, which will call for new applications of the story. The dialogue between text and community is clear.

Genesis-Numbers ←——→ Deuteronomy
Text (Old) ←————→ Community (New)

The result of this dialogue is also clear: Torah itself. Torah itself reflects the text-community dialogue. Moses becomes the authoritative reinterpreter of the past. As the histories of Judaism and Christianity demonstrate, Moses is not only the authoritative interpreter par excellence, but also the paradigm for all those who follow and who are called to engage in the same process. What is most significant, perhaps, is that the text-community dialogue is built into the structure of Torah itself. This pattern not only helps to explain the structure of Torah but also exemplifies a process that will characterize all subsequent Christian and Jewish communities. Even more important, all the remaining "additions" to scripture will mirror this same process, providing paradigms for the interpretation and role of scripture within the community of faith.

The following comparisons with Torah illustrate this observation.

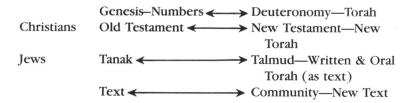

Here we see that the scriptures of both Christians and Jews continue the text-community dialogue and ultimately result in twofold canons reflecting the old (Tanak or the Old Testament) and the new (New Testament or the Talmud). It is not surprising or accidental that Moses is important for both the New Testament writers and the rabbinic sages, because they are in a very real sense continuing what he has begun.

The story is not yet complete. Throughout this study we have maintained that despite the authoritative nature of scripture the motivation
to interpret it comes from the contemporary community that experiences new revelations, new concerns, and new problems. Regardless
of the paradigmatic value of the text-community dialogue modeled in
scripture itself, interpretation and application of old promises and
stories are motivated by the contemporary community's need to live
out the biblical story in the present. That need often results in either
authoritative scriptures (e.g., the Writings) or in other authoritative
tradition when the canon is closed. Presupposing a closed canon, the
continuation of the text-community dialogue may be schematized in
the following way.

[Tanak➔Talmud]◄——►Tradition◄————————►Contemporary
                    (e.g., Maimonides)   Judaism

[O.T.◄►N.T.]◄————►Tradition◄————————►Contemporary
                    (e.g., St. Thomas)   Christianity

[Text➔Community]
              ↓
[New Text◄——Community]
                      ↓
[New Text◄————————►Community

This arrangement illustrates the common process of text-community
dialogue that characterizes Judaism and Christianity. It also illustrates
the differences between these scriptural communities. Despite the calls
for Christians and Jews to affirm a "common" (i.e., the Old Testament
or Tanak) scripture, the process of dialogue between text and community makes responding to those calls extremely difficult. If we begin
as members of a particular Christian or Jewish community, we cannot
reach our "common" scriptures except through the authoritative
traditions and the second part of our respective canons (Talmud or
the New Testament); that is, our dialogue with the text is mediated
through very different traditions and canons. We cannot dismiss those
traditions and still remain true to our contemporary communities. Our
purpose here is not to suggest that dialogue between Christians and
Jews on the subject of their scriptures is impossible. Rather, our tracing
of the text-community dialogue from Torah to the present day reflects
a commonly shared process, regardless of quite different results. However, by maintaining that such a dialogue always begins with the contemporary community of faith rather than with our common biblical

roots, differences—illustrative of a rich history of interaction between text and community—arise.

The Writings are an important part of the development into two separate twofold scriptural patterns for Judaism and Christianity.

Torah   New Testament
   &   Writings
Prophets   Talmud

Once again, the above pattern reflects both the common and the uncommon in the scriptural canons of Judaism and Christianity. The uncommon is clear enough. We have seen that the "writings" of early Judaism and Christianity were not the same (e.g., the acceptance of the apocryphal writings by the early church). Such differences may be seen as reflective of needs and concerns of ancient communities that chose and accepted different literatures as authoritative in light of their own particular experiences.

The common is equally clear. The Writings, when juxtaposed to Torah and Prophets, represent a continuation of the text-community dialogue. The ultimate twofold scriptural canons of Christians and Jews is dependent upon the paradigm of the Writings, for the Writings represent the first time this pattern is applied to scripture (Torah and Prophets) itself. Although we have found evidence for a text-community dialogue in earlier periods, its application to the scriptures of Judaism is found first in the Writings. Thus, the Writings point us toward Old Testament–New Testament or Tanak-Talmud canons. The dialogue between Torah-Prophets and the Writings is a microcosm of the ultimate dialogue reflected in the larger canons of Judaism and Christianity.

Although in one sense we may view the New Testament and the Talmud as further "writings," this is not entirely accurate when the final canons of Christians and Jews are examined. Ironically, the Writings almost disappear—becoming the least important canonical division for Jews and spread out throughout the Old Testament canon for Christians. Nevertheless, *when viewed as a whole* they witness to the centrality of a basic text (Torah and Prophets) and a fundamental interrelationship between that text and the community that uses it to ascertain the will of God and the mission of Israel, for the present and the future. What Christians and Jews finally share is not the scriptures found in Old Testament–New Testament or Tanak-Talmud. Rather, we share the often displaced or invisible texts of the Writings and the patterns of interpretation found within them. We share the process of responses made to Torah and Prophets that have become paradigmatic for all subsequent communities. The diversity of these responses becomes pluralistic once they are included in the canon. Such a canonical pluralism virtually guarantees that diversity will continue to characterize Christian and Jewish communities. It also demands that we share in the heritage of these post-exilic writers—trying to make sense of Torah and Prophets, even through many later revelatory experiences in the present day.

THE WRITINGS AND CANON

Although we have argued for the central importance of the Writings, the fact remains that for Christians this canonical division is not functional. Indeed, it is not to be found in their Bibles. If we wish to find the Writings as a canonical division, we must go to the Hebrew Bible or to its translations. For Christians the books of the Writings are spread throughout the Old Testament, sometimes with other "writings" (i.e., the apocryphal literature) added as well. In light of this development, some word of explanation, perhaps even an apologia, is needed. Why should not just Jews but Christians as well care about this canonical division?

Regardless of their ultimate place in the scriptural canon, a study of this post-exilic literature is essential for understanding the historical development of scripture. Moreover, the responses and developments this body of "writings" represents tells all Christians and Jews much about what it means to be a scriptural community, to be a people in dialogue with a book (Torah and Prophets). Further, the fact that this literature finally became scripture—authoritative literature—is true for both Christians and Jews, regardless of its present place within scriptural canons.

The Writings as a canonical division have much value for Christians. The fact that the present arrangement and collection of these books for Christians has its roots in the Septuagint and, for some, in the decisions of Reformers such as Martin Luther does not lessen the importance of our attention to this literature as a collection of diverse responses. To view the Writings together, as a whole, emphasizes the diversity of response and interpretation found in the Bible. Sometimes this rich heritage of diversity is blurred, even dismissed, when we look at one book, one response. The interaction within a scriptural community between many equally legitimate appropriations of the message of Torah and Prophets can be lost when all of these responses are not considered.

Through an examination of the diversity of the Writings as a collection, a better understanding and appreciation of the different places in which this literature is found in other, Christian, scriptural canons can be achieved. The diversity of this literature and the many ways it was used are responsible for the variety of ways it was collected by different communities of faith. We have argued above that the Writings provide a way of understanding and explaining subsequent intertestamental, New Testament, and rabbinic literature. The diversity of the Writings is continued, even intensified, when other collections of this material are examined and compared with it. If the organization of the Writings represents some attempt to collect this diverse literature by means of authorship (the Psalms), purpose (wisdom literature), function (Megilloth), or time (Ezra–Nehemiah, 1–2 Chronicles), the Christian canon represents the same concerns, with different results. Our purpose here is not to choose between one organization of canon and another, but simply to propose that the diversity of the Writings as a canonical division as well as the attempts to provide some rationale for their ultimate order is found in both Christian and Jewish canons.

Finally, the Writings as a canonical division is valuable for Christians in the sense that it is invisible, but not necessarily nonfunctional, in their present canons. The relative unimportance of most of this literature in the life of the church is at once a problem and at the same time reflective of the value, even the success, of these responses to emergent scripture. It is a problem only if we forget this body of literature altogether. The purpose of this study is at least in part to make such "forgetting" difficult. Yet, the Writings succeed in their attempts to tell us what it means to be a scriptural community when they are used, consciously or not, to affirm the pluralistic nature of scripture, when our attention is focused on the process of interaction between text and community they reflect. It is ultimately more important that we continue and participate in the process the Writings represent than that we know all the historical details of this literature itself.

The Writings, as a canonical division, point beyond themselves. Once in a while, it is essential for Jews and Christians to confront the diversity of this literature as a whole and to remember this essential function. The ultimate value of the Writings, when viewed as a whole, is in understanding what they *all* do, wherever they are found, and what, in many different ways, they call us to do.

Hence, before concluding this chapter, some observations about the unity of this literature are appropriate. Even if the primary value of this literature is to be found in the diversity it represents, all scriptural communities have tried to find ways to define the relationship among these writings and the other literature upon which they depend. Three possible ways of relating this literature to itself and to Torah and Prophets will be suggested. These are merely illustrative. Other ways are not only possible but also need to be found by biblical communities that continue the diversity of response found in Writings and that need to relate that diversity to scripture and to the larger bodies of which they are a part.

One approach would be to see the Writings as a variety of different ways to live the biblical story represented in Torah and Prophets. Thus, labeling each of the individual books as types of "living," the Psalms, Lamentations, and perhaps Esther, represent liturgical living; Ezra–Nehemiah and Chronicles represent establishment living; the wisdom literature represents practical living; and Daniel represents disestablishment living. Ruth and the Song of Songs could be either categorized within liturgical (or establishment) and practical living, respectively, or could be seen as special kinds of responses.

A second proposed organization would still evaluate the collection in light of Torah and Prophets. In such an approach the Psalms and its focus upon the worshiping community, the wisdom literature and its emphasis upon a reason-oriented approach to the created order, and, perhaps, Ezra–Nehemiah and 1–2 Chronicles with their focus upon Torah and the prophetic word in the midst of an established community—these three would constitute all important characteristics for subsequent communities of faith. Daniel and the Megilloth, however construed, would represent options and permutations available to, but perhaps not mandated by, every canonical community.

A third approach to the contents and organization of the Writings might use Mosaic and Davidic (royal) traditions as a starting point. Because these traditions are associated with different conceptions of the covenant and also are found, often in tension, in both Torah and Prophets, interrelationships between them found in the Writings would point to emergent scripture and the need for both parts of it to be central to the community of faith. As we have seen, the literature of Ezra–Nehemiah utilizes both Davidic and Mosaic traditions to establish the community and to point toward future restoration. The wisdom literature and the Psalms both have royal overtones and may be related to concerns of stability and of new revelatory activity found in Mosaic and Davidic traditions. Although explicit use of Mosaic and Davidic traditions is sometimes difficult to find in all the literature, the concerns for establishing the community, for eschatological hope, for prophecy—all of these can be related to the two major streams of tradition found in Torah and Prophets.

Two important characteristics of these syntheses need to be noted. First, it is the nature of the Writings that any synthesis will create tension. Thus, for example, to place Job, Ecclesiastes, and Proverbs together suggests that the very type of "living" or response represented by this literature will result in quite different interpretations of the same experiences and needs of the community. Such a synthesis highlights both the character of biblical diversity and the need to see all the alternatives within a common framework.

Second, no synthesis of the Writings will be a clean one; that is, although understanding the referential nature of this literature is important, it is also critical to ascertain that the task of synthesis is difficult and will often result in structures that give priority to one element over others. The factors that determine that priority are often extrinsic to the text and change from generation to generation, from culture to culture, and from faith community to faith community. Such a phenomenon is a testimony to the necessity for every faith community to continue to struggle with the canon and the structures found within it.

The Writings are ambivalent. They witness to the stability of the two other canonical divisions and at the same time suggest an open-ended approach to what it means to be a Torah-Prophets community. Although the particular texts contained in the canon of the Writings are agreed upon, the overall paradigm to which they point is open-ended, continually challenging and appropriating the "word" in a variety of ways. A primary concern of many biblical theologies is to search for a unity or a unifying principle. More often than not these searches have met with failure when tested by larger scholarly and ecclesiastical communities. On the synthetic level, no principle or theme seems to tie together these materials adequately and tightly. On the descriptive level the diversity is overwhelming. Perhaps the search for unity should be abandoned.

Yet, there is another option. What if we could systematize diversity? What if we could even find biblical precedent for this? This is what the Writings represent: the systematization of diversity. We have a canonical division, a "unity" of sorts—held together not by an internal cohesion but rather by the common texts to which they are a response.

This perspective takes seriously the fact that not only must canonization be presupposed to arrive at a final form but also the diversity within the division needs to be recognized as the product of many different communities over a long period of time. Although it is not the history that is being canonized but the paradigmatic responses to Torah and Prophets they represent, nevertheless, the theological richness and diverseness of the Writings are enhanced by the historical study in which we have engaged.

Such a view of the process that produced the Writings and of the function they have within the canon may serve as an important corrective to those who see the post-exilic period stereotypically: as a time when Judaism began a development that led to a sterile and rigid legalistic religion. A classic example for such a view is found in the following words of Wellhausen.

> When it is recognized that the canon is what distinguishes Judaism from ancient Israel, it is recognized at the same time that what distinguishes Judaism from ancient Israel is the written Torah. The water which in old times rose from a spring, the Epigoni stored up in cisterns.[4]

If we continue the metaphor, our study suggests that the water in the cisterns, represented by Torah, Prophets, and the Writings, creates a rainbow spectrum of color and choice in the light of new revelation for subsequent scriptural communities. Moreover, every scriptural community is mandated to continue the storing up process made paradigmatic by the post-exilic community. In addition to the different colors and the constant movement (contra Wellhausen) within the cisterns themselves, each community brings its own concerns and its new experiences of God to the process of determining the will of God and acting upon it. Our picture of the Writings and the post-exilic period that produced them testifies to a vibrant and multifaceted scripture that continues to provide a fecund and diverse heritage and challenge to all Jews and Christians.

Our study of the canonical division of the Writings witnesses to a historical process shared by all Christians and Jews—a common twofold scriptural pattern—*and* to different canons. We share a process that continues today, our heritage from the Writings. However, the Writings also help to explain differences; indeed, this important body of literature sanctions them. There is no one way to be God's people. There is no one way of ascertaining God's will valid for all and for all time. If, however, the Writings sanction diversity and help to explain the nature of a process that has led to different communities of faith with different histories, these often invisible books provide some hope for future interreligious and ecumenical dialogue as well. If we share the process of the past and our communities continue this process now, we also have the possibility, with the help of the God of Israel, of sharing more fully our differences and our commonness in the future. The composite message of the singers, sages, scribes, community builders, and seers who generated the Writings witnesses to such a possibility and calls us toward it.

7

Canon as Prolegomenon
for Theology

The purpose of this chapter is to explore some of the implications for
and potential contributions to a theological understanding of scripture
made by our hermeneutical analysis of the Writings and its development in Judaism and Christianity. It is important to state at the outset
that other areas besides theology, potentially just as significant, could
be explored; that is, the dialogue between community and a fixed
authoritative text that undergirds the Writings occurred and continues
to occur around many different topics and concerns. Although the
discernment of who God is and how the community of faith is to
define itself in relation to that God is of central importance, many of
the Writings themselves (e.g., Ruth, Esther, wisdom literature) are not
explicitly concerned with solely theological topics. The text-community dialogue can always be seen to point to God, but it can also
point to various aspects in the life of a people who have little apparent
interest in speaking "theologically." All of this is to recognize and
reiterate that the hermeneutic represented by the Writings is funda-
mentally a textual and social phenomenon. The theological implications of this phenomenon are great and integral to our total understanding of it, but other avenues might be explored as well.

The patterns of interpretation found in the Writings and the dynamic
interrelationship of text and community that produces these patterns
and legitimates still others in later times is set within the post-exilic
period of ancient Israel. As such, both the texts composed and the
process initiated are Jewish in their origin. The implications of this
provenance and the continuing textual interpretation by Jewish communities of faith witnessed to by the hermeneutic we have described
must be taken seriously by Christians who seek to study the theology
of the Old and New Testaments. The fact that Christians and Jews do
not now have the same biblical canon—regardless of a common starting

point and important hermeneutical similarities—must also be recognized. Thus, the first topics in our discussion of theology will focus upon the nature and identity of canon and the connection between Christians and Jews. After such a beginning, this chapter will devote its attention to issues that have most often been the concern of Christians, usually under the rubrics of Old Testament, New Testament, or biblical theology. Whether or not such issues are of import or significance to contemporary Jewish communities remains to be seen. In any case, the implications of the hermeneutic described in this study mandate beginning with Judaism and its connections with the early church.

An important proviso is necessary at this point. Twentieth-century Christians, heirs of the textual hermeneutics begun in the Writings and continued in Judaism and Christianity, begin their interpretation within particular and different communities from Jews and other Christians. Long histories of interpretation, regardless of the dynamic and dialogue between text and community that we share, also separate and differentiate us from one another. More important perhaps, the ways in which Christians and Jews view the hermeneutics or theology of their scriptures are colored by this long history of interpretation and the social and institutional history upon which it rests. Such observations necessarily qualify whatever hermeneutical or theological picture at which we arrive. Although the present study has attempted to trace a development beginning with the Writings and continuing to the present day, the contemporary problems, challenges, and revelations (e.g., pluralism, the Holocaust) are the real starting points for the hermeneutics described. Nevertheless, with this proviso firmly in mind, it is also the conviction of this study that all sorts and conditions of Christians and Jews share the very hermeneutical process that divides and separates them, a process begun in post-exilic Israel. The question, then, is not whether we can or should erase our particularity or the often horrid features of our history, but whether, today, we can continue together to participate in a text-community dialogue so central to all of us.

BIBLICAL OR CANONICAL THEOLOGY

One implication of the present study is that a better or more appropriate term to describe what has usually been called "biblical theology" might be "canonical theology." In order to justify such a terminological change, a brief review of the hermeneutical process begun in post-exilic Israel would be useful.

The Writings, the third section of the Hebrew Scriptures, point in many ways to a two-dimensional textual reality: Torah-Prophets (text) and Writings (community). Such a recognition is compatible if not congruent with recent scholarly observations that the primary textual divisions in post-exilic Israel are Torah and the "rest," however defined.[1] Ultimately, as we have seen, the dialogical process of text and communal response results in two-part canons: Old Testament–New Testament for Christians and Tanak-Talmud for Jews. Moreover, the dialogue begun in the Writings is frozen and made paradigmatic for future generations of Christians and Jews, suggesting that one primary characteristic and identifying component for both traditions will be an ongoing interrelationship between text and community.

Although many similarities and dissimilarities have been noted in Christian and Jewish canons, it is often in the authoritative traditions that follow the New Testament or the Talmud where problems seem to occur. Some Jews argue for an ongoing Talmudic, and thus canonical, tradition stretching to the present day; Christians do not. Nevertheless, Christians do connect many of their contemporary authority structures (for example, bishops) to phenomena or traditions found in their biblical canons. Regardless of the different ways in which Christians and Jews delineate their canons and maintain a continuing authority for contemporary interpretation (Oral Torah, apostolic succession, inspiration, and so forth), there is a common concern to connect the present community with the past, the new with old.

If, as we suggest, the hermeneutic that generates and maintains such a process is first to be seen in the development of Jewish and Christian canons, the term "biblical" appears inappropriate. The *Bible* is the canon for Christians, but not for Jews. In order to understand and include the full implications of the text-community dialogue begun in the Writings, "canonical" is the more appropriate term. The fact that the canons differ is not at issue, but rather it is the integrity of the hermeneutic that produces them.

Although we may continue to debate what is canonical for Jews, there is a basic reality common to Judaism and Christianity witnessed to by the choice of this term. Christians are able, if they wish, to try to bypass certain authoritative figures, but not the biblical canon. Jews may also attempt to discount Maimonides or Ibn Ezra, but not Tanak-Talmud, their canon. Indeed, the histories of both religions testify to such attempts to bypass such authoritative figures.

For the purposes of understanding and correctly representing the common origin of the text-community hermeneutic and the two-part authoritative textual traditions that result from it, serious consideration should be given to "canonical" versus "biblical" theology. Even if Christians continue to use the term "biblical theology," it is hoped that a growing awareness that this is only one part of a larger phenomenon, canonical theology, will occur.

THE JEWISH-CHRISTIAN CONNECTION

Within a more general call for Jewish-Christian dialogue on a wide variety of subjects (e.g., the Holocaust, the state of Israel) is found a concern to take the relationship of Christianity to Judaism seriously in the doing of biblical theology. In a recent work surveying the problems such a theology must address in the twentieth century, more than a third of the book addressed the relationship of Israel and the church.[2] In one sense, such a concern is not new at all, for the relationship between Old and New Testaments has always been a central issue for biblical theology and, in part, generates the present concern. Yet, the present climate among primarily (but not exclusively) Christians who deal with biblical theology is motivated by an increased and intensified awareness of the Jewish-Christian connection in light of the Holocaust and other contemporary phenomena.

Central to this contemporary concern, which hopes for increased dialogue between Christians and Jews and for a new perspective for biblical theology, are two separate but related mandates. First, the Jewish roots or background for Christianity must be studied in more depth and with more willingness to see the organic relationship between these theological traditions. As one scholar has recently stated in discussing the future of Old Testament theology, there is "a need to reposition the Christian movement within the much broader context of the emergence and consolidation of Judaism during the late biblical and early post-biblical periods."[3] Suffice it to say, such a concern stems from a contemporary recognition that too often Christians have ignored or disparaged early Judaism and focused attention on the normative theological message of the New Testament. The second mandate calls for an increased awareness on the part of Christians to the other Jewish authoritative tradition found in Talmudic and Midrashic literature.[4] Although the motivations for such a call are many, it is commonly recognized that contemporary theological understanding

and interfaith dialogue cannot occur if a critical part of Jewish interpretation and of the Jewish canon is ignored.

Such calls for a recognition of the Jewish-Christian connection in
biblical theology are not made naively; whatever positive outcomes
of contemporary dialogue might occur, there are deep theological
differences between Judaism and Christianity. Thus, many Old and
New Testament theologians rightfully continue to recognize, on the
one hand, the christological center of the New Testament and subsequent Christianity and, on the other hand, the lack of concern among
Jews to speak of the "theology" of Tanak or Talmud.[5] The realization
that religious Jews care less about Tanak than Christians do about the
Old Testament is often startling to both. In light of the rich and authoritative histories of Jewish and Christian tradition that are brought
to bear on the reading of scripture, a fundamental difference becomes
clear: in a very real sense, the Jewish Tanak and the Christian Old
Testament are *not* the same book; that is, in view of their very different
canons and histories, the theological and social value of this literature
is so different for Judaism and Christianity that some have rightly
suggested it is inappropriate to equate Tanak and the Old Testament.[6]

Beginning with the admission that the canonical hermeneutic we
have discovered in the Writings is itself motivated by some of the
contemporary concerns to make a Christian-Jewish connection central
for biblical-canonical theology, there are at least three ways in which
this hermeneutic affirms such a call and helps us deal with some of
the theological differences that divide us. First, the historical context
in which the interpretive patterns of the Writings emerged points to
the necessity of viewing Christianity as a part of a larger process
occurring within Judaism. Second, both the product (scripture) and
the process (community-text dialogue) are common to both sets of
traditions, then and now. Third, the theological diversity so much a
part of both Christianity and Judaism is not only found within the
earliest Jewish scriptural communities but also canonized for both
Christians and Jews in the final forms of their two-part canons.

Thus, the Writings and the hermeneutical process they initiate can
be helpful in current biblical theology and its concern for a Jewish-
Christian connection. This hermeneutic developmentally provides a
way to understand and explain the theological diversity among and
between early and contemporary Christians and Jews; it also points
to a common dialogue with a text, to be sure with very different
theological and social results. Canonically, this hermeneutic at one
and the same time justifies and condemns the theological diversity

found between Christians and Jews. It justifies inasmuch as the different theological interpretations all point to a common grappling with a shared authoritative tradition in the light of new revelations of God particular to specific communities. It condemns to the extent that adherents of particular revelations and new theological insight seek to exclude or even to silence other revelations and other ways of understanding who and what God is. Such attempts, unfortunately evident in both Christian and Jewish history, violate the pluralistic theological mandate of the canon. Central to the theological integrity and character of the canon is a dialogue between text and community, not a homogeneous and monolithic conception of either God or community.

To affirm the Jewish-Christian connection as fundamental for biblical-canonical theology is a primary consequence of the canonical hermeneutic set forth in this study. The Writings mandate a particular relationship between the book and the people, dialogical in nature. It does not demand the book be viewed in the same way, theologically, as the further development of Jewish and Christian canons amply illustrates. Indeed, one recent commentator has stated that the agenda of the rabbis was shaped more by the destruction of the Second Temple and its consequences than by Tanak study.[7] Surely a similar point could and should be made about the life, death, and resurrection of Jesus Christ for the church. Both sets of events have parallels with the various interpretive communities of the Writings, the experience of the exile, and its aftermath. What all of these phenomena share is the intermix of old (scripture) and new, resulting in theological and social diversity and new hermeneutics and values. All of this testifies to the fact that God cannot and will not be encapsulated in any one theological system: whether christological in nature, or in a constructive and systematic approach to the Old Testament or Tanak, or in the diverse words of the rabbis or sages. Each attempt to limit God not only is theologically impoverishing but also, from the perspective of the Writings and the canon, threatens to stop the continuation of a text-community dialogue that forms the basis of and provides the rationale for Jewish and Christian theology and dialogue.

WHICH CANON?

Although the canon and the hermeneutics associated with it argue for the importance of a Jewish-Christian connection for the doing of biblical-canonical theology, serious arguments have recently been made suggesting that the biblical canons of Christianity (the Septuagint) and Judaism (the Masoretic text) represent quite different views of scripture and of their function within its respective communities.[8] For example, the Masoretic text affirms the centrality of Torah in all of Tanak. Surely rabbinic Judaism can be viewed from such a perspective, suggesting that later interpretation must seen as parallel to Torah (Oral Torah). Likewise, the structure of the Septuagint with its emphasis on history and prophecy may be seen to view the latter as the culmination of the scriptural story. Thus, the New Testament becomes a continuation of this prophetic story or development with the Christ-event as the normative lens through which Christians read that story. These arguments rest upon an analysis of the different structures of these biblical canons as well as upon the recognition that scripture is viewed differently by Christians and Jews.

Many have argued for the theological significance of the tripartite division of Tanak for Christians. Others maintain that the Masoretic text is and must remain the primary scriptural witness for Christians and Jews.[9] The issue at hand is whether the differences between the Septuagint, arguably the scripture for most early Christians, and the Masoretic text are so significant that a hermeneutic based upon canon must choose between them. If a canonical hermeneutic leads to such a dichotomy, then it is not very helpful at all.

We have suggested above that the Septuagint is not a problem for but rather a confirmation of the canonical hermeneutics we have discerned in the Writings. Basic to the arguments for different canons and views of scripture is a diversity of opinion about the role and function of Torah and its relationship to the prophetic traditions. The Writings themselves confirm such a view, as a comparison of Ezra–Nehemiah and 1–2 Chronicles readily demonstrates. Moreover, regardless of whether we accept the traditional views concerning the development of Torah, Prophets, and Writings, or whether we see Torah first and then the "rest" prophetically conceived, clearly there were many ways to resolve or live with the tension between Torah and the Prophets in post-exilic Israel.

From a chronological perspective, it would appear that the septuagintal text and the reading of scripture it represents are developments that occur after most of the Writings are composed. As such, the Septuagint reflects as a whole the very dynamic found within each of the Writings, namely, the appropriation of scripture by a contemporary faith community. It can certainly be argued that prophecy is not the only significant factor that determines the structure of the Septuagint and that wisdom and other communal interpretive traditions already found within the Writings have a role as well. Even if a relatively monochrome understanding of Tanak or the Septuagint is accepted, however, the picture of post-exilic Israel and of the hermeneutics found within it and epitomized by the Writings adequately explains both canons.

In light of our contemporary concern for a Christian-Jewish connection, Tanak appears to be the most significant starting point for a discussion of canon, its hermeneutics, and their theological implications. Such a starting point must not downplay the diversity and differences represented by the Septuagint or the Masoretic text, however. Such diversity is embraced by both canons and ultimately rests on the text-community dialogue that produced them and the larger canons of which they are a part. The final question is not "whose canons" or "which canon," but how will we understand the nature of a scriptural community that tries to live faithfully in accord with mandates of the "old" and in light of the "new"? Neither Tanak nor the Septuagint provides the definitive answer for Christians or Jews. Yet, the hermeneutic they both reflect and urge upon us suggests a common task and a common God. As such, they represent two variations on one canonical theme.

CANONICAL HERMENEUTICS REVISITED

To this point we have focused upon the implications of an interpretation of canon for the scope and terminology, the interrelationship of Christianity and Judaism, and the identity of the text used for a theological analysis of the authoritative canons. The purpose of the present section is to explore the implications of our study of the Writings and subsequent developments for constructing a theology of scripture. To date, most of this work has been done by Christians under the rubrics of Old Testament, New Testament, or biblical theology. Perhaps this will continue to be primarily a Christian enterprise, but the implications discussed below do have import for Jewish-Christian dialogue on a number of topics in the future.

Our study of the Writings focused on the needs of post-exilic communities and the functions that scripture (Torah and Prophets) had within those communities. The particular literary ways in which scripture was used were then examined, revealing a wide and sometimes divergent variety of theological interpretations. When canonized, these interpretations became a pluralistic paradigm sanctioning diversity in later Judaism and Christianity. Central to our presentation was the observation that a dialogue between a common text and the community of faith characterized all of the Writings and what followed. Our study confirms the recent statement of Rowan Greer, commenting upon later developments in early Christianity, themselves dependent upon the process begun in the Writings.

> Text and interpretation are like twin brothers; one can scarcely tell the one from the other. What emerges is an unbroken dialogue or discourse between a book and a people, between Scripture and tradition, between the letter and the spirit, between word and the experience of those hearing it.[10]

Moreover, this study affirms one basic task of biblical theology, namely, to reflect "on the coherence of subject matter of the Christian faith in the mutual critical interpenetration of traditional and contemporary experience."[11]

It is important to note that, although the present canons of both Jews and Christians point in their structure and content to the basic dialogue between scripture and community, the hermeneutics discovered are first precanonical, although presupposing an authoritative text.[12] The present study has chosen to describe these post-exilic hermeneutics in theological ways. Much more remains to be done before a unified or systematic theology of the scripture or canon can be achieved. James Barr has rightly seen one productive contribution of canonical hermeneutics to biblical theology when he states that canonical study might provide:

> an account of the dynamics and development of canon and canonical form, which would serve as preparatory material for theological evaluation; the theological evaluation, however, would have to handle the canonical material thus described in a critical and evaluative way, that is, it would not be constrained to follow the lines of the canon as described.[13]

The implications of the "preparatory material" embodied in this study for the doing of biblical theology will now be discussed in an abbreviated and illustrative manner. Permeating this discussion is the recognition that theology is not merely a descriptive or constructive task; it has a confessional component as well, whether Christian or Jewish in origin. The statement of K. H. Miskothe concerning Jesus applies equally well to Jews, with a change in point of reference: "To know *who* he is, is the ground of the church. *What* he is, we must be constantly taught afresh by the Torah and the prophets."[14]

Problems and Task

It is widely recognized today that biblical hermeneutics and theology must address the interrelationship between the theological enterprise and historical-critical method. As James Sanders has aptly pointed out: "It is the task of biblical hermeneutics today to seek a midpoint between the hermeneutical task of the historical-critical method (seeking original meanings) and the hermeneutical task of spanning the gap between recovered norms and modern cultural systems of meaning."[15] This study maintains that historical criticism is vital for providing a picture of the origins of a text-community dialogue while also recognizing that the canon itself, by making all of the canonical interpretations pertinent and applicable to communities of faith, goes far beyond the intentions of any particular community as discovered by historical study. Historical criticism should not be used to determine the most authentic, earliest and best, "theology." It can be helpful, however, in determining the "final" theological proclamation of the canon. At least from the perspective of this study, historical criticism can be used in the analysis of post-exilic Israel to locate the beginnings of a text-community dialogue and the various theological interpretations set forth. No judgments about which of these interpretations is "best" can be made at this point, although the final perspective of canon does suggest norms and guidelines. The continuing task of evaluating and determining the most appropriate theological interpretations of the Writings or other scripture for current faith and practice, to the extent to which it does not violate the theological diversity of the canon, remains for later theologians and their communities.

One apparent problem inherent in the hermeneutical picture presented here is that of historical relativism. With a strong focus on the needs of particular communities and insistence that all hermeneutical activity begins in the contemporary setting, how can the text be seen to maintain its ability to speak "objectively"?[16] Further, how is it that any community can be challenged and corrected? Where is the authority of scripture for all communities?

One of the implications of canonical hermeneutics for biblical theology is a recognition of theological relativism.[17] No one picture of God is normative above all others. No one interpretation of scripture can adequately provide answers to the questions of identity and mission. Indeed, the canon in its final form provides the justification for such a relativism. Biblical authority for all communities rests in part on a social reality roughly parallel to and congruent with such a

canonical theological reality. That is what keeps us honest. What makes
the Bible or Tanak-Talmud authoritative for all is the existence of many
different communities, each with its own different theological perspectives grounded in the canon, constantly challenging and critiquing
each other and continuing to engage in a text-community dialogue.
Such a picture of biblical theology and authority is at once freeing and
dismaying. It is the heritage of the canon; yet, it implies no one has
all the truth about God.

A canonical hermeneutic contributes just this to the ongoing debate
about the "descriptive" and "constructive" tasks of biblical theology.
The hermeneutics traced in this study have required both descriptive
and constructive procedures. It follows that any theological analysis
that takes canon seriously will be both descriptive and constructive
in nature. It will be descriptive to the extent that the particular theological perspectives of each community are presented primarily on
their own terms as found in the biblical texts. However, the framework
of the canon is itself a construct and not the only possible framework
for theology. How do we view such a construct theologically? What
theological priorities are assigned to the canon as a whole? How will
we relate the many different theologies to each other and to the canon?
These questions and others point to the need for a constructive approach to biblical theology. Further, they suggest that canonical hermeneutics alone are unable to deal with the rich theology of the
scriptures. Although the canon can provide a starting point and important guidelines, other methods and perspectives, constructive and
systematic in nature, are necessary to deal with the issues raised by
the canon.

Structure

Of what theological significance is the tripartite structure of the Hebrew canon or Tanak? Several possibilities present themselves as a
result of our study. Does the canon provide a way to understand and
structure the theology of the whole? Do the larger sections of the
canon contain distinguishable theological categories for such a task?
Does the canonical structure of Tanak help us to understand the nature
of the relationship between Old and New Testaments, always a central
concern of biblical theology? Going in another direction, does the
canon's structure generate the problem? By grouping diverse and divergent theological perspectives in what often appears to be nonsys-
tematic ways, does the canon raise issues of diversity and pluralism

that the more systematic and constructive goals of theology must deal with?

These questions have been given many answers, ranging from a complete rejection of the canon and its structure as hermeneutically significant to calls for canon to be the starting point for all biblical theologies. For example, John Barton has recently stated:

> So for all attempts to find a hermeneutical significance in the fact that certain books are in the canon, or in their assignment to one "division" rather than another, have turned out to be a wild goose chase.[18]

Then again, Brevard Childs and others continue to argue that the canonical shaping of individual books and larger units is of great significance for the doing of biblical theology.[19] A correct assessment of the value of canonical structure for theology probably rests somewhere between these extremes. The purpose of this section is to discuss briefly the possible significance of canonical structure for the theological task while realizing many other factors are also important. The fact that Childs himself has used the concept of intertextuality to understand the relationship between the different canonical theologies he finds in biblical literature is a testimony to the need for other, noncanonical perspectives and methods in the overall task.

The tripartite structure of Tanak has been seen as important for many contemporary Old Testament theologians. Such an observation is not new, however.[20] The motivations for taking canonical structure seriously have been varied. Sometimes the structure is mentioned only to dismiss its pertinence. For example, the different levels of authority associated with these divisions in Judaism have led to a dismissal of significance simply because it is Jewish and the task of "Old Testament" theology is Christian. More often, Old Testament theologians have sought to find ways to describe the theological message of the Old Testament on the basis of its Tanak structure. Thus, the structure of Torah, Prophets, and Writings is seen to reflect the saving plan of God as promised, realized, and developed,[21] or as determined by the word of God and response in historical, prophetic, and didactic ways.[22] In these and other theologies, categories (soteriological, historical, literary, and so forth) are used to locate and organize what is most central to the overall theology of each canonical division.

Although such presentations have great value and surely point to the importance of canon and its structure for theology, more often than not choices are made that exclude or devalue certain theological messages within the canon.[23] The implications of the canonical hermeneutics found in this study provide an important perspective from

which to view the contemporary task of biblical theology and suggest
at least one other approach may be of value. Recently, Joseph Blenkinsopp has said in reference to the post-exilic literature: "It is an
irony that Old Testament theology cannot accommodate those writings
which, in theme and procedure, most closely approximate theology
as we recognize it today."[24] In light of our study, such an observation
has great implications for the future of Old Testament or biblical
theology. Perhaps, taking seriously the tripartite structure of the canon
and its hermeneutical significance, one of the future tasks of biblical
theology is to present, in separate studies or in a larger work, a picture
of the theologies of the Writings as, so to speak, the "first" biblical
theologians. Such a presentation would not focus on the "Kerygma"
of these writers, as earlier works of biblical theology in this century
have done. Rather, the central concern would be to discern how the
authors of the Writings constructed their theological message by responding to a central and authoritative textual corpus, much as biblical
theologians today must do. Such an approach would be inclusive rather
than exclusive, using the canon as determinative for which books or
theologies should be included, and with Torah-Prophets as the primary
text. Such a theological presentation would be at once a mirror of
what the Writings have done theologically and a paradigm for what
we must continue to do. Surely some envision a further need to systematize and to find theological norms, but the implications of canonical hermeneutics would suggest that first all books must be included and seen as a critical part of a text-community dialogue before
such judgments are made.

Finally, the development of the New Testament as presented in our
study has important implications for the future of biblical theology.
Happily, some scholarship has addressed this issue already.[25] Whether
we view the New Testament as further "writings" or apply other hermeneutical and theological norms to this literature is not clearly determined by a canonical hermeneutic alone. What is mandated, however, is the placement of the New Testament literature within the
larger framework of Jewish scriptural interpretation that results in
both a Christian and a Jewish canon. Without such a framework, the
theological issues raised by the New Testament will not be dealt with
accurately or in a way that reflects the nature and scope of its message,
in all its particularity and its commonality with Judaism. The structural
similarities between the testaments may offer some valuable insights
in the future. For example, we might ask whether the New Testament

contains within itself a structure (Gospels parallel to Torah, Epistles to Prophets) to which later Christian tradition is the "Writings."

Implications for Current Issues

Two current issues in biblical theology are the problems of unity-diversity and particularism-universalism. These issues are chosen to demonstrate the contributions of a canonical hermeneutic for biblical theology. Certainly canon can be important for many other issues, but our purpose is illustrative in scope.

In a very real sense, the canon generates the problem or issue of unity and diversity. Whether viewed as open or closed, as Christian or Jewish, there is *one* canon for any particular faith community. Yet, within that canon is a diversity of theological perspectives that, because of the authority attributed to the canon as a whole, as one, cry out for interrelationship. Often, as we have seen, such an interrelating occurred in the biblical period itself. Indeed, at least at the level of Torah-Prophets and Writings and their subsequent development, that interrelating is made normative for all subsequent biblical communities. Viewed in this way the canon not only generates the problem but also identifies a central task for all who have the canon.

Responses to this canonical problem of unity and diversity have been many. Some, with the help of categories found within the canonical divisions themselves, have affirmed diversity itself as a major theological norm. On the one hand, although no complete canonical theology has been produced to date, such a theology would inevitably need to focus on many theological perspectives as normative rather than one. On the other hand, the diversity of the canon is sometimes seen to set the challenge. Where *is* the unity? What *is* the oneness of God to which all of these diverse theologies testify?

Several different answers have been given, none of them entirely satisfying.[26] Yet, at least three implications of the canonical hermeneutic presented here help to shape a solution of this issue. First, any resolution should neither harmonize away nor disguise the diversity of the canon. Such a procedure goes against the canonical witness itself. Second, any appeal to the unity of the biblical theological witness, whether through a focus on the oneness of the canon or God, will inevitably be tension-filled because it will be forced to leave something out or to devalue it. Such a procedure is not entirely illegitimate, for surely the authors of the Writings did this. In view of the canon,

however, contemporary theologians must at least recognize the tensions created. Finally, and this observation is a corollary of the second
point, no systematic or constructive presentation of theological unity
can be a clean one, a picture that does not leave gaps or holes. As we
have suggested above, this dilemma is not only or primarily a reflection
of being honest with the canon but, more important, an insight about
the nature of the biblical God.

The issue of particularism and universalism can be related to the
diversity of theological witnesses in the canon, for surely this diversity
results from the reflection upon God and an authoritative text within
particular communities. Unfortunately, particularism is often viewed
in pejorative terms by contemporary theology. For example, Judaism
is seen to be a very particularistic religion, whereas Christianity is a
universal religion. Recent attempts by theologians to focus on creation
are in part reflective of the negative evaluation of particularism. If God
is God of all, how can we speak of a particularistic God? Although
these attempts to find universalistic elements within the canon are
surely to be commended, the implications of the canonical hermeneutic traced in this study suggest another way to approach this problem, a way that embraces rather than rejects particularism.

The process of textual interpretation that ultimately produces both
Jewish and Christian canons is particularistic in the extreme. The
authors of the Writings, the New Testament, and the rabbinic literature
all must be set within their very specific communities. When this is
done, we can no longer speak of a Christian universalism and a Jewish
particularism, but rather of Christian and Jewish particularism, sometimes in conflict with each other, sometimes in conflict within each
"body." The canon, which contains many different manifestations of
this particularism, is not a mandate for Christians or Jews to be all
things to all people. Rather, it is a mandate to recognize that God has
been, is, and will continue to be particular things to particular people.
Further, all of this is the story of God and God's people. What we share
is our own particularity, but, for Christians and Jews at least, this
particularity is based upon and the result of a common dialogue between authoritative text and community.

Only after such a recognition may we dare to use universality as a
concept pertinent to the canon. The activity of God can indeed be
affirmed as universal but only when all of the particular ways in which
God is active are seen. At that point the oneness of the canon can
indeed be used to reflect a universal God, much as the individual

instruments of a symphony orchestra may reflect the unity of a complex musical composition.

Interrelationship with Other Methods

Reviewing here all the methods that have been used to construct theologies of the Old Testament, New Testament, or the Bible would be impossible. Nevertheless, it is fair to say that most theologians who have attempted to produce such biblical theologies have tried to find a key element or elements within the biblical texts themselves, as well as some systematic framework for the presentation of their particular theology. Often insights, categories, or paradigms from other disciplines have played a significant role in the shape or function of the theology produced. All of this is not only unavoidable but also reflective of the very process discovered in the Writings, although none of these early authors had as their goal a systematic presentation of God in the whole biblical text.

Some contemporary theologians find the key to the construction of a biblical theology in a particular conception of God, in a series of hermeneutical developments, in major themes, in central concepts, or in developmental schemes. In all of these, the canon can be helpful. It may set the parameters for theological evaluation or help to identify important themes and hermeneutics.

When all is said and done, however, biblical theologians will in all probability need more than just the canon or its hermeneutics to construct a theology. Two recent theological treatments that take seriously some of the implications of the canonical hermeneutic found in this study may be mentioned for illustration only. Hermut Gese has approached biblical theology through a history of traditions approach. Maintaining as this study has that the canon of the Writings was open at the time of the New Testament, he traces a history of revelation witnessed to by the development of scripture.[27] Although his starting and ending points are explicitly Christian and therefore do not see the wider implications witnessed to by the parallel developments of the Jewish canon, there is much compatibility between his approach and ours. Again, Claus Westermann has presented an outline of Old Testament theology that takes seriously the structure of the Hebrew canon and the categories of "Word" and "response."[28] Although his own conception of "Word" forces him to relegate certain parts of the Writings to a lesser status, nevertheless, the basic dynamic found in his categories holds much in common with the canonical hermeneutic presented here. If one controlling concept were to be chosen for biblical theology on the basis of our study, it would probably be "word."

A broader implication, already mentioned above, for theological methodology applied to the Bible has to do with the relationship of any systematic or dogmatic approach to the descriptive task. Our analysis of a canonical hermeneutics, at a descriptive level, affirms diversity and relativizes any attempt to find an overall theological system. At the same time, by virtue of its wholeness, the canon also demands that we attempt to find the elements that unify it. For a time, historical criticism was often used either to affirm diversity and particularity or to search for the most authentic theological meaning or concept in the Bible. Fortunately—and the recent focus on canon as authoritative text within a community of faith has much to do with this—many biblical theologians affirm the need for a descriptive approach and the value of historical study, while at the same time recognizing that larger, often systematic, theological approaches must be brought to bear on the task of biblical versus systematic theology. To the extent that such attempts reflect a careful dialogue between the contemporary community and its needs with an authoritative text, the task, if not the agenda and the methods, of biblical theology is congruent with the canon and its own intentions.

TOWARD THE FUTURE

The preceding discussion of the possible implications and contributions of a canonical hermeneutic for the future task of biblical or canonical theology has two conclusions. First, an interpretive framework based upon canon does raise new problems as well as clarify old ones, suggests certain starting points, and helps to define the value of certain methods and agendas pertinent to the theological endeavor. Second, a canonical hermeneutic by itself is not sufficient for the construction of any theology of scripture or canon. Rather, the canon and the process that produced it witness to the need for other disciplines and their perspectives.

Such needs can be related to either the text or community sides of the canonical process. In order to hear the text speak in its particularity and its universality, there is a need for continued interfaith, ecumenical, and intracommunity dialogue. Without all of these, we will be unable to hear the canonical text speak with its fullest authority and in its rich theological diversity.

In order to hear the community speak, with all its needs, challenges, and new revelations, we need to be sensitive and open to a wide variety of disciplines and perspectives speaking on every possible theological and social issue. Only by such an openness will the community be able to bring its own needs and concerns into honest and full dialogue with the biblical text.

The results of this study, tentative and fragile in nature, call for further work in the history of the post-exilic, New Testament, and rabbinic periods, for further sociological study of the nature of those communities, and for more dialogue with systematic theologians, philosophers, and literary critics. Only with the help of all these disciplines and others will the full implications of the canon for theology be understood and made applicable. In some cases, these other disciplines and their perspectives will, I hope, confirm and add to the results of our study. In other cases, important correctives or qualifications will occur. For example, the recent focus on the importance of orality and the warnings that a religion of the "book" may be a distortion of the ancient evidence represent important perspectives that call for further study of the development and function of scripture and canon.[29]

The canon demands continued dialogue in a pluralistic context between authoritative text and community. This is its mandate. The matrix upon which such a pluralism rests is not a particular conception of God but rather the common dialogue between a text, conceived and valued in many different ways, and a wide variety of very particularistic communities. In and through all of this, God is made known, and the people find their identity and mission.

In the title of this chapter, canon was referred to as a prolegomenon for theology. Such a title claims that canon and the hermeneutics associated with it represent one essential perspective for future theology. It also suggests that much more needs to be done both from the perspective of canon itself and with the help of many other disciplines. One hopefully enduring characteristic of the canon is its comprehensive, pluralistic nature. This characteristic demands inclusion of Jews and Christians and of many disciplines and perspectives for the task of theology. Ultimately, of course, as our study of the Writings has shown, the canonical witness is concerned with far more than how to do theology. Rather, with its affirmation that many have been given glimpses of God's purpose and none has the entire, complete, and final answer, the canon calls us to continue to study the text—bringing our problems, disappointments, and joys to it. Only through such a process, inclusive of all, can we discern and act upon the Word of God in our midst. This is the witness of the authors of the Writings and the heritage of the canon they helped to shape.

Notes

1. Introduction

1. See, for example, Brevard Childs, *Old Testament Theology in a Canonical Context* (Philadelphia: Fortress Press, 1985), 1–19.

2. Although it was several centuries before the Jewish and Christian canons were complete, we may speak of the formation of a textual community beginning at this time. See, for example, Jacob Neusner, *Canon and Connection: Intertextuality in Judaism*, Studies in Judaism (Lanham, Md.: University Press of America), 4ff., for the distinction between "communities of texts" and "textual communities." Although this study is ultimately concerned with both, we now refer to the former.

3. Diversity as a problem in current biblical theology is discussed again in chapter 7.

2. Canon and Interpretation

1. See Brevard Childs, *Biblical Theology in Crisis* (Philadelphia: Westminster Press, 1970), and James Sanders, *From Sacred Story to Sacred Text* (Philadelphia: Fortress Press, 1987). The bibliography in Sanders's book is especially helpful.

2. See "Cave 11 Surprises and the Question of Canon," *McCormick Quarterly*, 21 (1968): 284–98.

3. See D. F. Morgan, "Canon and Criticism: Method or Madness?" *Anglican Theological Review*, 68 (1986): 83–94.

4. *Old Testament Theology in a Canonical Context*, 192.

5. See, for example, his treatment of the canonical structures and message of individual biblical books in *Introduction to the Old Testament as Scripture* (Philadelphia: Fortress Press, 1979).

6. See "Adaptable for Life: The Nature and Function of Canon," in *From Sacred Story to Sacred Text*, 9–39.

7. See *Torah and Canon* (Philadelphia: Fortress Press, 1972), 50–53.

8. For example, James Barr, *Holy Scripture: Canon, Authority, Criticism* (Philadelphia: Westminster Press, 1983), 156–57.

9. *Introduction to the Old Testament as Scripture*, 96.

10. See *Old Testament Theology in a Canonical Context*, 13.

11. Ibid., 55.

12. For a more general but similar position that suggests the laws of Torah must be read in light of the narratives that precede them, see David Weiss Halivni, *Midrash, Mishna and Gemara* (Cambridge, Mass.: Harvard University Press, 1986), 9–17.

13. Ibid., 16.

14. Such criticisms are unfair, for all of Childs's work is permeated with a sophisticated knowledge and use of traditional historical-critical methodology. However, because he is not motivated by values and goals often attributed to these methods ("original" as best or most authentic, etc.), he is sometimes seen, wrongly, as eschewing them altogether.

15. See his general statements about canonical criticism and its components in *Canon and Community* (Philadelphia: Fortress Press, 1984) as well as his more specific treatment of Torah in *Torah and Canon*, 1–53.

16. See J. Sanders, *From Sacred Story to Sacred Text*, 21ff.

17. Ibid., 89; and *Canon and Community*, 77–78.

18. For the Old Testament, see his *Introduction to the Old Testament as Scripture*. For the New Testament see *The New Testament as Canon: An Introduction* (London: SCM Press Ltd., 1984).

19. See "Canon and Criticism: Method or Madness?" 93–94; and James Barr, *Holy Scripture: Canon, Authority, Criticism*, 91.

20. *Old Testament Theology in a Canonical Context*, 192.

21. For a discussion of intertexuality and its potential import for the study of rabbinic material, see *Canon and Connection*.

22. See, for example, *Canon and Community*, 43f.

3. Community Shapes the Text

1. See, for example, *From Sacred Story to Sacred Text*, 26–29, 111–14.

2. John Barton, *Oracles of God. Perceptions of Ancient Prophecy in Israel after the Exile* (London: Darton, Longman and Todd, 1986), 44–95.

3. For example, Roger Beckwith, *The Old Testament Canon of the New Testament Church* (Grand Rapids: William B. Eerdmans Publishing Company, 1985), 63ff.

4. So Sanders and many others; see *From Sacred Story to Sacred Text*, 65.

5. James L. Kugel and Rowan A. Greer, *Early Biblical Interpretation*, Library of Early Christianity, edited by Wayne A. Meeks (Philadelphia: Westminster Press, 1986), 57.

6. *From Sacred Story to Sacred Text*, 11–39.

7. One example of the inability of any "system" to explain all of the biblical books adequately is pertinent at this point. The present chapter does not deal with the Song of Solomon, although it is clearly a part of the Writings. The

difficulty involved in identifying a community and an agenda to be associated with this book is responsible for this omission. Although we could deal with this book under the present guidelines and concerns, it would stretch the evidence, and therefore we have chosen not to discuss it at all.

8. See, for example, James L. Crenshaw, "Prolegomenon," in *Studies in Ancient Israelite Wisdom,* edited by J. L. Crenshaw, Library of Biblical Studies, edited by Harry M. Orlinsky (New York: KTAV Publishing House, 1976), 1–60.

9. See, however, Robert Gordis, "The Social Background of Wisdom Literature," *Hebrew Union College Annual,* LVII (1943/44): 77–118; and Brian Kovacs, "Is There a Class Ethic in Proverbs?" in *Essays in Old Testament Ethics,* edited by J. L. Crenshaw and J. Willis (New York: KTAV Publishing House, Inc., 1974), 171–89, for two examples of attempts to define and locate the social locus of this literature.

10. For an analysis of the importance of scribes in the Deuteronomic movement, see Moshe Weinfeld, *Deuteronomy and the Deuteronomic School* (Oxford: Clarendon Press, 1972).

11. See Michael Fishbane, *Biblical Interpretation in Ancient Israel* (Oxford: Clarendon Press, 1985).

12. John Bright writes, "There was a danger that if the community could not pull itself together, regain its morale, and find direction, it would sooner or later lose its distinctive character, if not disintegrate altogether. Drastic measures were needed, for the community could neither continue in its present ambiguous situation nor could it recreate the order of the past. Some new path would have to be found if Israel was to survive as a creative entity," in *A History of Israel,* 3d ed. (Philadelphia: Westminster Press, 1981), 379.

13. See, for example, Paul Hanson, *The Dawn of Apocalyptic* (Philadelphia: Fortress Press, 1975).

14. See, for example, Paul Hanson, *The People Called: The Growth of Community in the Bible* (San Francisco: Harper & Row, 1986), 299–300, 310–11.

15. See D. J. A. Clines, *The Esther Scroll: The Story of the Story,* Journal for the Study of the Old Testament, Supplement Series, 30 (Sheffield: Journal for the Study of the Old Testament Press, 1984); and Jack M. Sasson, *Ruth* (Baltimore: Johns Hopkins University Press, 1979).

16. See *Ruth;* and S. Talmon, "Wisdom in the Book of Esther," *Vetus Testamentum,* XIII (1963): 419–55.

4. The Text Shapes Community

1. See Leo G. Purdue, *Wisdom and Cult,* SBL Dissertation Series, 30 (Missoula: Scholars Press, 1977).

2. See D. F. Morgan, *Wisdom in the Old Testament Traditions* (Atlanta: John Knox Press, 1981), 142ff.

3. Note that these roles are dependent upon reading the text as it presently stands, rather than on the basis of a reconstructed history of the period.

4. J. Sanders, *Torah and Canon,* 113.

5. Continuity of the Scriptural Pattern

1. Paul Hanson, *The People Called,* 332.

2. John J. Collins, *Between Athens and Jerusalem* (New York: Crossroad, 1983), 15.

3. *The People Called,* 350.

4. *Between Athens and Jerusalem,* 15.

5. *The People Called,* 338.

6. E. P. Sanders, *Paul and Palestinian Judaism* (London: SCM Press Ltd., 1977), 424.

7. James H. Charlesworth, "Introduction for the General Reader," in *The Old Testament Pseudepigrapha* (Garden City, N. Y.: Doubleday & Company, 1983), vol. 1, xxix.

8. Ibid., xxiv.

9. Although the Talmud is the largest and arguably the most important part of the rabbinic writings that form the second major division of the Jewish canon, other writings are usually included as well (cf., for example, *Canon and Connection,* 15–28). Although we will discuss some of this other literature, when we refer to the two-part Jewish canon for the sake of convenience we will designate it as "Tanak-Talmud." However, the reader is urged to keep in mind the other authoritative literature of the sages.

10. James Charlesworth, *The Old Testament Pseudepigrapha,* vol. 1, xxviii.

11. Besides the work cited above, see also *The Old Testament Pseudepigrapha* (Garden City, N.Y.: Doubleday & Company, 1985), vol. 2.

12. See, for example, David Winston, *The Wisdom of Solomon* (Garden City, N.Y.: Doubleday & Company, 1979), 14–69.

13. See *Between Athens and Jerusalem,* for an examination of this literature.

14. Gerald Sheppard, *Wisdom as a Hermeneutical Construct,* Beihefte zur Zeitschrift für die alttestamentliche Wissenschaft, 151 (New York: Walter de Gruyter), 82.

15. See, for example, Hermann L. Strack, *Introduction to the Talmud and Midrash,* Harper Torchbooks (New York: Harper & Row, 1965), 12ff.

16. In light of the importance of the sages and their voluminous literature, it is probably better to understand the *Midrashim, Mishnah,* etc., as a new form of "wisdom" now given to the people. Although the form and content are radically different in light of the developments we are tracing, the function of this new literature is congruent with the aims of many earlier wisdom writers.

17. See *Oracles of God.*

18. See *Paul and Palestinian Judaism,* 419–28.

19. *The New Testament as Canon: An Introduction,* 32–33.

20. See *The Old Testament Canon of the New Testament Church,* 110–80.

21. See, for example, Walter Bauer, *Orthodoxy and Heresy in Earliest Christianity,* edited by R. A. Kraft and Gerhard Krodel (Philadelphia: Fortress Press, 1971).

22. *The New Testament as Canon: An Introduction,* 31.

23. See, for example, Norman Perrin, "Eschatology and Hermeneutics," *Journal of Biblical Literature,* 93 (1974): 3–14.

24. On the development of a bipartite New Testament canon and the parallels with "Law and Prophets," see W. Schneemelcher, "General Introduction," in Edgar Hennecke, *New Testament Apocrypha,* edited by Wilhelm Schneemelcher (Philadelphia: Westminster Press, 1963) 1:32ff.

25. More often than not, "scripture" (i.e. Tanak) refers only to the first part of the Jewish canon. The implications of this different nomenclature are discussed in chapter 7 below.

26. In "Forward for Jews," in *The Old Testament Pseudepigrapha,* vol. 1, xii.

27. *Paul and Palestinian Judaism,* 72.

28. *Introduction to the Talmud and Midrash,* 9–10.

29. James Kugel, "Two Introductions to Midrash," *Prooftexts,* 3 (1983): 143.

30. *The People Called,* 350.

31. Elias Urbach, *The Sages: Their Concepts and Beliefs* (Jerusalem: Magnes Press, 1979), vol. 1, 568–69.

32. Jacob Neusner, "The Virtues of the Inner Life in Formative Judaism," *Tikkun,* 1, no. 1 (1986): 77–78; emphasis added.

33. *Introduction to the Talmud and Midrash,* 11.

34. Jacob Neusner, *Midrash in Context* (Philadelphia: Fortress Press, 1983), 136–37.

35. *Paul and Palestinian Judaism,* 180; emphasis added. For a critique of this characterization, see *From Athens to Jerusalem,* 13ff.

36. Jacob Neusner, *Messiah in Context* (Philadelphia: Fortress Press, 1984), 229.

37. Ibid., 230–31.

38. For a detailed discussion of the taxonomy of the rabbinic canonical material, see *Canon and Connection,* 95–144.

39. Besides Beckwith, see S. Z. Leiman, *The Canonization of Hebrew Scripture: The Talmudic and Midrashic Evidence,* Transactions of the Connecticut Academy of Arts and Sciences (Hamden, Conn.: Archon Books, 1976), 47.

40. *The New Testament as Canon: An Introduction,* 19.

41. See *The Old Testament Canon of the New Testament Church,* 382–95, and the secondary literature cited there.

42. *Midrash in Context,* 135–36.

6. The Writings as Canon

1. See *Orthodoxy and Heresy in Earliest Christianity*.

2. *The New Testament as Canon: An Introduction*, 25–26.

3. Leonhard Rost, *Judaism Outside the Hebrew Canon*, translated by David Green (Nashville: Abingdon, 1976), 24.

4. Julius Wellhausen, *Prolegomena to the History of Ancient Israel* (Cleveland: Meridian Books, 1965), 410.

7. Canon as Prolegemenon for Theology

1. See *Oracles of God*, 35–95.

2. Henning Graf Reventlow, *Problems of Biblical Theology in the Twentieth Century*, translated by John Bowden (Philadelphia: Fortress Press, 1986).

3. Joseph Blenkinsopp, "Old Testament Theology and the Jewish-Christian Connection," *Journal for the Study of the Old Testament*, 28 (1984): 11–12.

4. See, for example, *Problems of Biblical Theology in the Twentieth Century*, 121, citing the work of Rosemary Ruether.

5. See Matitahu Tsevat, "Theology of the Old Testament—A Jewish View," *Horizons in Biblical Theology*, 8, no. 2 (1986): 33–50; and Jon D. Levenson, "Why Jews Are Not Interested in Biblical Theology," in *Judaic Perspectives on Ancient Israel*, edited by J. Neusner, B. Levine, and E. Frerichs (Philadelphia: Fortress Press, 1987), 281–307.

6. For example, J. F. A. Sawyer, "A Change of Emphasis in the Study of the Prophets," in *Israel's Prophetic Tradition*, edited by R. Coggins, A. Phillips, and M. Knibb (Cambridge, Eng.: Cambridge University Press, 1982), 245.

7. William S. Green, "Scripture in Rabbinic Judaism," *Horizons in Biblical Theology*, 9, no. 1 (1987): 31.

8. See, for example, J. F. A. Sawyer in *Israel's Prophetic Tradition*, 244-45. Many others have made similar observations about the differences in the role and function of scripture reflected in the Septuagint and the Masoretic texts.

9. See *Old Testament Theology in a Canonical Context*, 10.

10. *Early Biblical Interpretation*, 157.

11. G. Ebeling, quoted in *Problems of Biblical Theology in the Twentieth Century*, 165.

12. See Gerald T. Sheppard, "Canonization. Hearing the Voice of the Same God through Historically Dissimilar Traditions," *Interpretation*, 36 (1982): 28.

13. *Holy Scripture: Canon, Authority, Criticism*, 170.

14. Quoted in *Problems of Biblical Theology in the Twentieth Century*, 59.

15. *From Sacred Story to Sacred Text*, 65.

16. See Erhard Gerstenberger, "Canon Criticism and the Meaning of *Sitz im Leben*," in *Canon, Theology, and the Old Testament Interpretation*, edited

by G. Tucker, D. Petersen, and R. Wilson (Philadelphia: Fortress Press, 1988), 29.

17. See the recent comments by Paul Hanson, "Biblical Interpretation: Meeting Place of Jews and Christians," in *Canon, Theology, and the Old Testament Interpretation*, 32–47.

18. *Oracles of God*, 82.

19. See *Old Testament Theology in a Canonical Context*, 13.

20. See, for example, Joseph Blenkinsopp, "Old Testament Theology and the Jewish-Christian Connection," *Journal for the Study of the Old Testament*, 28 (1984): 3–15; and H. G. Reventlow, *Problems of Old Testament Theology in the Twentieth Century*, translated by John Bowden (Philadelphia: Fortress Press, 1985), 97.

21. The position of E. Stakemeier, referred to in *Problems of Old Testament Theology in the Twentieth Century*, 97.

22. Claus Westermann, *Elements of Old Testament Theology*, translated by D. W. Stott (Atlanta: John Knox Press, 1978), 10.

23. Thus, for example, Westermann has difficulty giving serious attention to wisdom literature in light of his system. See Ibid., 11.

24. "Old Testament Theology and the Jewish-Christian Connection," 6.

25. See the works of James Sanders and Brevard Childs as well as other scholarship cited in *Problems of Biblical Theology in the Twentieth Century*, 10-144.

26. For an apologetic for the systematic task of Old Testament theology as well as a beginning attempt at it, see Rolf Knierim, "The Task of Old Testament Theology," *Horizons in Biblical Theology*, 6, no. 1 (1984): 25–57; and "On the Task of Old Testament Theology," *Horizons in Biblical Theology*, 6, no. 2 (1984): 91–128.

27. See, for example, his *Essays on Biblical Theology*, translated by Keith Crim (Minneapolis: Augsburg Publishing House, 1981), especially 9–33.

28. *Elements of Old Testament Theology*, especially 9-34.

29. See William S. Green, "Scripture in Rabbinic Judaism," *Horizons in Biblical Theology*, 9, no. 1 (1987): 26–40; and Walter J. Ong, *Orality and Literacy: The Technologizing of the Word* (New York: Methuen, 1982).

Ancient Sources

Old Testament

GENESIS			15:5	64
1	60		21:29	64
1-12	72		23:26ff	64
12-50	72		28:8	62
EXODUS			2 CHRONICLES	60, 64ff., 86, 92
1-18	72		1:3	64
19-Numbers	72		5:7	64
			5:10	64
DEUTERONOMY	21, 29, 41, 72,		7:18	64
101, 121			8:13	64
6:20-25	60		24:6	64
23:4ff.	68		25:4	64
25:17-19	70		30:16	64
			35:12	64
RUTH	2, 6, 8, 49ff.,		36:22	67
	68ff., 99			
4:18	69		EZRA	2, 6, 7, 8, 31, 35,
				40, 44ff., 51f., 78,
1-2 SAMUEL	44			84ff., 101
			1.1	67
1 SAMUEL			2:2	67
15:7-9	69		3:2	65
			3:4	65
1-2 KINGS	44		3:10	64
			5:11	64
1-2 CHRONICLES	2, 35, 40, 44ff.,		6:18	65
	84, 98, 101f.		6:19	65
			7:5	65
1 CHRONICLES	64ff.		7:6	65
2:9-15	69		7:10-11	65
6:1-19	64		8:20	64
6:31-48	64		9:1	65
12:17	64		9:7	65
15:4	64		10:3	65

NEHEMIAH	2, 6, 31, 35, 40, 44ff., 51f., 78, 84ff., 101
1:7f.	65
3:16	65
7:7	70
8:1	65
8:13	65
8:14	65
8:18	65
9:3	65
10:28ff.	65
12:37	65

ESTHER	2, 8, 42, 49ff., 68ff., 99
2:5	70
4:1	70
6:12	70
9:29-32	70
9:30	70

JOB	2, 40ff.
14	60
28:20-28	59

PSALMS	2, 18, 35f., 40, 42ff., 61ff., 92, 101
1	43
37	43
49	43
85:8-13	62
95:7-11	62
119	43

PROVERBS	2, 40ff., 52
1:20ff.	60
2	114

8	114
8:22-31	59

ECCLESIASTES	2, 40ff., 83
3:16-22	60

SONG OF SOLOMON	2, 70, 72, 92

ISAIAH	92
24-27	47
51:12-16	60
56-66	47

JEREMIAH	
25:11	67
29:10	67

LAMENTATIONS 2, 42ff., 62ff.

DANIEL	2, 7, 8, 42, 47ff., 52, 66ff., 70, 78, 99
1-6	47f., 85
2-7	47
2	47
4:10	67
4:22	67
7-12	48
9	47, 67
9:24-27	67, 98

HOSEA	
14:9	61

JOEL 47

ZECHARIAH	
8:19	70
9-12	47

Apocrypha

1 Esdras	86
2 Esdras	86

Tobit	86
Judith	86

Additions to Esther 86

Wisdom of Solomon 60, 82, 85, 92

Ecclesiasticus 18, 36, 85, 92, 103
24:23 61, 85

Qumran 81ff.

Baruch 85

Letter of Jeremiah 86

Prayer of Manasseh 85

1-2 Maccabees 84, 86

Other Literature

Pseudepigrapha 81ff.

New Testament

Luke
24:44 92

Acts 94

Revelation 94

Authors

Barton, J., x, 141, 149
Barr, J., 4, 138, 148, 149
Barth, K., 11
Bauer, W., 152
Beckwith, R., 149
Blenkinsopp, J. x, 142, 153, 154
Bowden, J., 153, 154
Bright, J., 150
Bultmann, R., 11

Campenhausen, H., von, 93
Charlesworth, J., 83f., 151
Childs, B., ix, x, 4, 8, 11ff., 17, 22, 24ff., 91, 93, 116, 141, 148, 149, 154
Clines, D. J. A., 150
Coggins, R., 153
Collins, J., 151
Crim, K., 154

Ebeling, G., 153

Fishbane, M., 150
Frerichs, E., 153

Gerstenberger, E., 153
Gese, H., 145
Gordis, R., 150
Green, W., 153, 154
Greer, R., 138, 149

Halivni, D., 149
Hanson, P., 4, 150, 151, 154
Hennecke, E., 152

Knibb, M., 153
Knierim, R., 154
Kraft, R., 152
Krodel, G., 152
Kugel, J., 149

Leiman, S., 152
Levenson, J., 153
Levine, B., 153

Miskothe, K. H., 138
Morgan, D., 148, 150

Neusner, J., 148, 152, 153
Noth, M., 5

Ong, W., 154
Orlinsky, H., 150

Perdue, L., 150
Perrin, N., 152
Petersen, D., 154
Phillips, A., 153

Rad, G. von, 5
Reuther, R., 153
Reventlow, H. Graf, 153, 154
Rost, L., 153

Sanders, E. P., 101, 151
Sanders, J., x, 4, 8, 11ff., 22ff., 34, 38, 139, 148, 151, 154
Sasson, J., 150
Sawyer, J. F. A., 153

Schneemelcher, W., 152
Sheppard, G., 151, 153
Stakemeier, E., 154
Stott, D., 154
Strack, H., 151

Talmon, S., 150
Terrien, S., 4
Tsevat, M., 153

Tucker, G., 154

Urbach, E., 152

Weinfeld, M., 150
Wellhausen, J., 153
Westermann, C., 4, 145, 154
Wilson, R., 154
Willis, J., 150
Winston, D., 151

Subject Index

Apocalypse, 47, 74
Apocalyptic Literature, 2, 47ff., 66ff., 85ff.

Biblical Ethics, 66
Biblical Theology, 2, 4, 6, 8, 29, 131ff.

Community Builders, 44ff., 53ff.
Canon, 4ff., 11ff, 18ff.
  authority of, 18
  canon within canon, 16f.
  Open or closed, 36, 79ff., 103ff.
Canonical Hermeneutics, 4ff., 19ff., 134, 137ff.
Canonical Theology, 131ff.
Canonization, 22, 37, 104ff.

David, 2, 41, 45f., 50f., 62, 64ff., 69, 92
Deuteronomic Movement, 35, 41, 60
Deuteronomistic History, 46, 61
Diversity, 6f., 26, 33f., 113f., 118, 143f.
Dialogue between text and community, 5, 7ff., 13ff., 17, 19f., 26ff., 39ff., 55ff., 94, 110, 121ff.

Edifying Literature, 68ff., 85ff., 116

Former Prophets, 64ff., 69f., 72

Historical Literature, 64ff., 85ff., 115f.

Jerusalem, 45, 64f., 77
Jews and Christians, 2f., 10, 29, 106f., 110, 122ff., 130f., 133ff.
Joseph, 49, 51, 67, 69

Latter Prophets, 72
Liturgical Literature, 61ff., 85ff., 115

Megilloth, 118f.
Midrash, 22, 44, 66, 97ff.
Moses, 2, 21, 19, 36, 38, 41ff., 49, 64ff, 121

Particularism, 144f.
Pluralism, 6, 12, 26, 76ff., 110ff.
  canonical, 6, 111ff.
  cultural, 6, 76ff., 111ff.
  religious, 111f.
  scriptural, 6, 76ff., 90, 111ff.
Post-Exilic Period, 9, 30ff.

Relativism, 139f.

Sage, 10, 40ff., 49ff., 53ff., 67, 75ff.
  rabbinic, 40, 42, 99ff.
Sapiential Literature, 59ff., 85ff., 114ff.
Septuagint, 47, 50, 105ff., 135ff.
Singers, 42ff., 53ff.
Storytellers, 49ff., 53ff.

Talmud, 10, 96ff.
Tanak, 6, 10, 103
  as canon, 21, 80, 104, 135ff.

Unity, 143f.
Universalism, 144f.

Visionaries, 47ff., 53ff., 68

Wisdom Literature, 2, 7, 40ff.
   see also sapiential literature